8-19-63

The Layman's Role Today

The
Layman's
Role
Today

FREDERICK K. WENTZ

DOUBLEDAY & COMPANY, INC.
GARDEN CITY, NEW YORK
1963

Grateful acknowledgment is made for permission to use the following material:

Abingdon Press for selections from two articles by Frederick K. Wentz which appeared in *Religion in Life* for Spring 1960 and Spring 1962.

Association Press for selections from *To Be a Man* by Robert Spike and *Christianity and the Social Crisis* by Walter Rauschenbusch.

Excerpt from "Poverty, Piety, Charity and Mission" by William Stringfellow from May 10, 1961 issue. Copyright © 1961 Christian Century Foundation. Reprinted by permission from *The Christian Century*.

Dr. Clair M. Cook for description of the career of Dr. William N. Keith.

J. Curwen & Sons, Limited, London, for "A Blessing" by Martin Shaw.

Creating Christian Cells (Revised, 1960) is published by Faith at Work, Inc., 8 West 40th Street, New York 18, N.Y., and is priced at 75¢. Used by permission.

Houghton Mifflin Company as the original publishers of *The Poetic and Dramatic Work of Robert Browning*.

Alfred A. Knopf, Inc., for selections from *A Simple Honorable Man* by Conrad Richter.

The Laymen's Movement for selections from *The Laymen's Movement Review*, November–December 1961.

The Lutheran for selections from articles by Frederick K. Wentz which appeared in the issues of March 30, 1955; October 17, 1956; June 18, 1958; October 18, 1961; for selections from "Man on the Spot" by Herman G. Stuempfle, Jr., which appeared in the issue of January 4, 1961; selections from an article by Frederick K. Wentz which appeared in *Resource*, December 1961.

The Macmillan Company for selections from *Prisoner for God* and *Cost of Discipleship* by Dietrich Bonhoeffer, and *Ecumenical Era in Church and Society* by Edward Jurji, ed.

National Council of the Churches of Christ in the U.S.A. for selections from an article by Frederick K. Wentz appearing in *The International Journal of Religious Education*, November 1958.

"The Scripture quotations in the publication are from the *Revised Standard Version of the Bible*, copyrighted 1946 and 1952 by the Division of Christian Education, National Council of Churches, and used by permission."

From "For the Time Being" by W. H. Auden, copyright 1944 by W. H. Auden. Reprinted from *The Collected Poetry of W. H. Auden* by permission of Random House, Inc., and Faber and Faber Ltd., London.

Dr. John Oliver Nelson for the 1962 "Style-of-Life" of Kirkridge.

The Westminster Press for material by Frederick K. Wentz from *Crossroads*, January–March, 1960. Copyright © 1959 by W. L. Jenkins. By permission.

The World Alliance of Young Men's Christian Associations for "The Agony of God" by Georgia Harkness, which appeared in *World Communiqué*, May–June 1960.

World Council of Churches, for selections from "Called to Unity" by Joseph A. Sittler (published in *The Ecumenical Review*, January 1962, Vol. XIV, No. 2). Department of Studies in Evangelism for CONCEPT I, George Webber's description of worship in his East Harlem Protestant Parish; Department on the Laity for selections from *Laymen's Work*, June 1954, Spring 1955, June 1956; from *Laity*, November 1957, February 1962.

The author wishes to express appreciation and indebtedness to the following persons for ideas, illustrations, and critical comment which have helped materially in the writing of this volume: Samuel Emerick, Julia A. Lacy, Werner Simpfendoerfer, Herman G. Stuempfle, Jr., Abdel Ross Wentz.

TO
Mani, Lisa, Ted, Melanie

CONTENTS

SECTION ONE

The Need for a New Layman

CHAPTER I

THE DILEMMA OF TODAY'S LAYMAN

Doing the Split

"If all the men here took your words seriously, Pastor, what on earth would you do with us?" Dick Leonard said this in a casual way as he shook hands after the service, but he was quite serious.

His pastor had just challenged the men of the congregation to serve their Lord and church more fully. Dick knew from experience that this meant being willing to usher, to serve on the council and committees, to teach in Sunday school or sing in the choir, and to help with visitation programs. If all the men were to volunteer, the pastor would be swamped.

What really bothered Dick was not the pastor's problem but his own sense of frustration in his church life. He didn't feel that he could add to his services to "Lord and church" that way. He was pretty much involved in responsibilities at home, at his work and with his service club. Besides, his talents were along other lines: as a technician he was wrapped up in his tasks as a machine serviceman.

Dick Leonard's sense of frustration is typical of the church experience of many American laymen today. And there's the other side of their experience, typified by an event in Harry Rohrbaugh's life.

Harry is a paint salesman and an active, conscientious

member of his church. But there came the Friday when his boss confronted him with a new consignment of paint to be sold and announced bluntly, "Harry, we're stuck with this stuff; it's just not up to specifications. But we've got to sell it, because we can't afford a total loss as big as that. Get it out to your regular customers next week." That weekend Harry was almost sick about his coming week's work. He thought about arguing with the boss or simply refusing or warning his steady customers. He went to Sunday school and church, and it made him feel better, but it didn't help him at all to find the wise and Christian thing to do on Monday. Nor was Harry at all sure that a talk with the pastor would help clear things up. He could think of a lot of phrases from the Bible and from sermons, but none of them quite seemed to fit.

As a paint salesman Harry Rohrbaugh has little support or guidance from the church for making Christian decisions. The modern Christian who would be a conscientious churchman finds himself living in two separate worlds. There is a sharp split between his church experience and the rest of his life, a widening chasm between his religion and his daily existence.

An able young woman who was well educated and broad in her interests was willing to serve in her congregation. She talked to the minister and the president of the Women's Society, hoping she could teach, or help with programing, or take part in a study group. She actually felt rebuffed when asked to be chairman of knitting for the bazaar.

Examples could be multiplied. Here is an outstanding astronomical physicist who takes it for granted that his active churchmanship shall consist of ushering and serving as deacon. Here is the microbiologist of international fame who finds easy entry into many influential places as a scientist; yet as a churchman his role for his mission congregation is that of making evangelism calls in homes where he often finds only reluctant entry as another eager denominational representative. And then there is the construction boss who regularly takes command of a crew of workmen, handles the men in fair and friendly fashion, and turns out a good day's production. But in church he has throughout years of loyal attendance remained passive and silent because he does not easily express ideas or readily address a church group. Such men can find no connection between the two roles they play. They can find no real challenge for their skills in the church's programs. They are left with a schizophrenic pattern of life and are tempted to conclude that religion belongs in an airtight, separate compartment, unrelated to the most vital areas of life.

Some laymen are quite conscious of this chasm and never seek to bridge it. Said one active churchman in North Carolina: "I never try to apply what I learn and affirm on Sunday to my job during the rest of the week." This was an unusually bold declaration, but it is not uncommon for modern Christians to deny by their acts and attitudes that Christ is Lord in their workaday world. Many a businessman is convinced that he'd go bankrupt in six months if he applied Christianity to his business. Recently, some Americans who claimed they considered religion something "very important" were asked, "Would you say your religious beliefs have any effect on your ideas of politics and business?" Fifty-four per cent answered "no."

It may be that there are church people who are not bothered by the fact that they think and act one way on Sunday and another way during the other six days. They may not care much about integrity. They may even refuse to notice that they believe one thing when they are being religious and believe quite the opposite when they are working or playing. It may not seem important that they can on occasion fervently claim, for example, that all men are their brothers and yet in the daily routine regularly reject or ignore or sneer at certain individuals or ethnic groups.

Surely, however, most churchmen need a sense of integrity, some unity and wholeness as persons. These people regularly live under a tension between their commitments in the church and their commitments in the world. This has always been true for the Christian; but in America today that tension is so great—because the gap between church and world is so vast—that few can bear it in a constructive manner. Most lay people, men and women, fall into a crippling compromise. In addition to the laymen who do not face the dilemma at all, there are four patterns of compromise which can readily be seen.

Four Ways to Compromise

There are hosts of churchmen who simply conform to the actions and habits and decisions of the people who surround them. They live by the world's patterns. They may withdraw entirely from an organization which asks them to profess or to do what they cannot carry out. Or they may maintain nominal membership but refuse to listen to the church any further. Many signs indicate that, whereas the tide of religious enthusiasm swept people into the churches in the 1950s, the ebb will carry away large numbers of the lukewarm or uncommitted church membership in the 1960s. In any case, it is those who remain on the lists of active members who make it possible for a sociologist to state quite accurately that "church members hold the same values as everybody else, but with more emphatic solemnity."

Others, who are more intent upon really being Christians, make a distinction between their spiritual life or inner decisions, on the one hand, and their participation in material things or their outward involvement in environment and society, on the other hand. They try to walk into the complex and tightly organized necessities of daily life protected and guided by an inner aura of individual piety and a set of purely personal moral standards.

The whole trend of American Christianity for several centuries has led to this particular pattern for relating Christians to the world around them. Pietism and revivalism have so shaped Christians in America that they take it for granted that they are to serve Christ in their daily activities with a very minimum of church authority or discipline or theology to direct them. Nor is it important to participate in an organized and informed way in the politics and power plays and structured organizations of society. Christians have the right inner life, and all would be well if others had it too.

Typically a Christian businessman with this viewpoint will consider God his silent partner, to be consulted in prayer, in listening to private conscience, in Bible verses, and in personal judgments. But this businessman will not expect God to have anything to say about his business transactions by speaking through other interested parties, through opposition blocs, through informed fellow Christians, through the writings of Christian ethicists, and through the myriad facts in the case.

A third pattern of compromise in trying to reduce the tension between church and world is much like the second and is perhaps more common. It is the distinction between the private area and the public area of life. This Christian identifies family, home, and church as his personal life, where he is expected to act like a Christian. Quite distinct is the arena of daily work, political decisions, and civic responsibilities. Here one is expected to maintain other standards, whether these be the law of the jungle or the canons of respectability. Recent decades have uncovered quite a few examples of established churchmen, good family men of considerable civic stature, who have maintained illegal and destructive monopolies or built homes that were substandard and shabby. As Peter Berger puts it, "The person listening to the minister in church is a radically different one from the person who makes economic decisions the next day. . . . As soon as he steps outside the charmed circle of church, family, and suburban neighborhood, he may become a tyrant, a ruthless exploiter of men, a participant in any number of merciless conspiracies—and no one 'back there' need ever know."[1]

This pattern also has roots that lie deep in historic Christianity in America. The Protestant Reformers sought to replace monasteries with Christian homes as the workshops of real piety. Each man was expected to serve daily as priest in his own household. Congregational life, aside from the corporate worship on Sunday at eleven, has grown up since the eighteenth century as an adjunct to the Christian home. It is within the home-congregation axis that Christianity has been nurtured in America. No wonder that women have taken to this pattern more aggressively than men! In recent decades the role of the home in American society has been shrinking and the influence of the public sector (commercial entertainment, huge corporations, large-scale education, massive government) has steadily increased its dominance. A religion that relates convincingly to the private and personal side of life but not to the public areas and the social structures will increasingly tear apart its laymen (particularly its men).

The fourth pattern of compromise is more rare but more visible within church life. It is often lauded extravagantly —the escape into religion. Those who are obsessed with religion or preoccupied with church activities become the

[1] *The Noise of Solemn Assemblies* (Garden City, Doubleday, 1961), pp. 37–38.

heroes and leaders among churchmen. It is assumed that the more one is devoted to religious matters, the more Christian he is. Or it is felt that the more time one spends in the church, the better churchman he is. Logically, under such assumptions, the ideal person would be a religious fanatic entirely withdrawn from the world. Most American Protestants are far from being withdrawn fanatics and would quickly reject that as the ideal, yet in their church life they continue to harbor this assumption: the more preoccupation with religion and church, the better.

That is why there are men in nearly every class of our theological seminaries who are ministerial candidates for the very odd reason that they have decided to take their Christianity seriously. Some of them are older men who have turned from successful careers in business or teaching. They have been told not only that stewardship consists of contributions to church budgets and that evangelism means bringing new members into the congregation but also that the Christian vocation or calling is into full-time church occupations, preferably as clergymen. One wonders how many thousands of our young people have decided that they can be only halfhearted Christians because they are unable to envision themselves as clerics or as religious fanatics.

Recently, when the commanding officer of a large airfield became a candidate for the ministry he was quoted as saying, "The layman can serve God and the Church in many ways, but I felt *I had to do more.*" "Why," asks his biographer, "did he decide to take up the way of the cross on a *full-time basis?*" (Italics added.)[2] Who can really say that the average clergyman does more for Christ or travels the way of the cross more nearly full-time than the man responsible for a large military airfield? Without judging the

[2] Quoting from Francis O. Ayres, *The Ministry of the Laity* (Philadelphia, Westminster, 1962), p. 17.

rightness of this individual's personal decision, one can point out that uncritical praise of such a step encourages the fourth kind of compromise, namely, escape into religion.

Why Belong to Church?

Behind the widespread acquiescence in this fourth compromise lies a basic confusion about the purpose of church membership. Why does one belong to the church? What does it really mean to be a church member, whether laity or clergy?

Some would say that they are churchmen in order to get into the next life. As Charles Wesley put it:

> A charge to keep I have,
> A God to glorify,
> A never-dying soul to save,
> And fit it for the sky.

But this sentiment, taken alone, is self-seeking and introverted, quite in contrast to Christ's admonition that he who would find his life must first lose it. Christians are not those who escape into religion and soul-cultivation. Christians are people who, for Christ's sake, live with other people and for them.

One Scotch theologian finds the "saved" quality of life evidenced in the prostitute who was dancing with a sailor when a drunken shipmate lunged at her partner with a murderous knife. This girl spontaneously threw her body before the flashing weapon, giving herself to protect her companion.

Churchmen preoccupied with religion and their souls cannot evidence the "saved" quality. They are not ready to lose themselves in service to human need.

Religious fanaticism does not help anybody. Eugen Rosenstock-Huessy tells of a woman who busied herself with

reading theology and converting people, becoming so immersed in religious activity that she made a nuisance of herself. One day her pastor "had a serious talk with her and
told her that religion had become a cancer in her system.
'Cut it out!' he suddenly shouted. She was dumfounded, of
course, but obeyed his orders, left the Church, secularized
her life completely, and became an enterprising horsewoman
who was liked everywhere."[3]

Actually, most modern church members, even the loyal
ones, are not overly religious. Nor do they really sing that
stanza of Wesley's hymn with any fervor. They have not
thought much about glorifying God. They have something
else in mind in church on Sunday (and the rest of the week).
Nor have they really figured out what the soul is or how it
is fitted for the sky.

At any rate, these churchgoers could probably sing more
accurately—even though Wesley *did not* write it—like this:

> To help my church to grow,
> Its programs to fulfill,
> O may it all my powers show
> And keep my conscience still.

People join the churches because they want to identify
themselves within the community. They need quick-growing
roots since they move frequently. They want a sense of belonging. They are anxious to have fellowship and to get
into the swing of social activities. It is expected of each
American that he will identify himself as a Jew or a
Catholic or a Protestant of some denomination.

Perhaps underneath this near-compulsive participation in
programs is a nagging sense of guilt. Many a church worker
is trying to atone for his guilt by his good works in the
drudgery of routine church tasks. He is trying to purchase
"cheap grace" through services to a good cause. He wants to

---

[3] *The Christian Future* (New York, Scribners, 1946), pp. 125–26.

quiet his conscience and to escape the tensions of Christian living by burrowing into a strenuous round of religious activity. He loves his church as any religious man loves his idol or symbol—to be taken care of because it is taking care of him.

H. H. Walz, German churchman, tells of a recent experience in America when he met a man of whom his pastor and fellow church members appeared quite proud. He was "the lay champion of his church." With due modesty he told Walz how he was spending six evenings a week in some church organization. "Having discovered on inquiry," Walz states, "that he was married and had three children, and that he was a businessman and a Republican, I said I hoped that from now on he would find the time to spend five evenings out of the six with his family, with his hobbies, with his business colleagues, and his political party, all of which need a good Christian much more badly than any church organization."[4]

Charles Wesley did write a second verse to that hymn. For many Christians today it would seem to present a shocking shift in emphasis. Actually it is right on target as an expression of the real purpose of churchmanship:

> To serve the present age,
> My calling to fulfill;
> O may it all my powers engage
> To do my Master's will!

In later chapters the meaning of this purpose for modern Christians, in terms of a style of life, will be spelled out a bit. First, however, it is necessary to point out that the dilemma is found not only in the experience of the layman. Nor is the confusion only in the thinking of the layman. The posture of the church itself in modern society poses the problem on a larger scale.

[4] *Laymen's Work*, June 1954, p. 1.

CHAPTER II

THE PLIGHT OF TODAY'S CHURCH

The Parish Ghetto

In our day a great gulf yawns between the organized churches and the rest of modern civilization. Church ideas and programs are remote from the surrounding world. Our churches have become too much a world of their own, a whirl of religious activities, a preoccupation with "things of the spirit" and the fellowship of the worshiping clique. The wheels of ecclesiastical machinery are whirring; but they do not mesh with the daily routines of men. Though religion is quite popular in America, it does not affect daily decisions or alter the social fabric. The church has been pushed into a ghetto.

There are many reasons for this. As a whole, the church has not kept pace with modern society. City life, industrialization, rapid technological advance, the vastness and complexity of modern society—these have left the church behind. She is discontented with their existence and unable to meet their questions. One is reminded of the little lady who sells picture cards at the formal Riverside Drive entrance to the Interchurch Center in New York. Few people pass that way and few are seeking cards, whereas the Claremont entrance is crowded with people, many of whom could use the help of an information lady. The church often appears to be where the people are not, offering services that do not meet the most pressing needs.

For example, the church continues to offer help (and rightly so) in the perennial cycle of birth, marriage, children, sickness, and death. But she has not yet learned to work through the secondary experiences of twentieth-century people—irregular work habits, mobility, high living standards, clubs and voluntary groupings, class alignments, leisure-time habits, etc. Yet modern men are often most readily and vividly reached within these ever-changing patterns of an industrial civilization.

The attitudes of many people in modern society also leave the church on the periphery of contemporary life. It can be summed up in the word secularism. The typical modern man is secular in a thoroughgoing way. He cannot really believe in the supernatural, in a God who stands above the world in power and purpose. For him this world and this age are the whole of it, and he must try to "squeeze life between two dates on a tombstone." He may have a wistful desire to be possessed by some ultimate. He may join a church seeking an answer. But he can seldom experience God's presence there. Usually his attention is focused upon purely human hopes and ambitions. The inner faith of a Christian fellowship is entirely lost on him.

Many a man outside the church must look at it as the person on the station platform sees the train that rolls through the station without stopping. Just a few feet away one can see people reading and chatting and eating, but they are entirely sealed off, quite removed, intent upon unknown destinations.

The Introverted Church

What is worse, the churches often seem to want it that way. The ghetto seems to be self-imposed. The churches appear to be intent upon a separate life and their institutional security without concern for the people and conditions that surround them. This has been called church-narcissism, self-admiration. There is a dangerous tendency for church organization with the churchmen in it to love and serve itself, sucking ever more people and resources into the contemplation of its navel and the decoration of its nave.

Too many congregations have an "edifice complex," bending all energies to raise a building that will be impressive and comfortable for their own prestige and enjoyment. The church is supposed to be the Body of Christ. Yet, as Paul Van Buren asks, "Is this how Christ treated his body, wrapping it up in stained glass, multithousand-dollar organs, and thick carpeting?"

Too often a congregation acts like a club, a voluntary association of like-minded people. The clergyman is hired to arrange the club's programs and to provide certain spiritual services for the membership. Only the right type of person is really welcome to join.

Even stewardship easily becomes a matter of self-concern and institutional maintenance. Recently a denomination's national stewardship office distributed a packet of materials under the theme "His Love . . . My Response." Of the thirty-two items in the packet, only six mentioned anything about service beyond organized church activities. Under the heading "Christian Stewardship of Time and Abilities," a card stated that "Christian Stewardship is the *practice* of the Christian religion" and listed forty-eight ways a person might go about practicing the Christian religion. Forty-one of the forty-eight items were listed under the heading "Congregational Life." Four were under "Personal" and three under "Family and Community." Faithful attendance at congregational meetings got as much attention as all of one's responsibilities in daily work. All of family life got but one item—to "hold family devotions."

Such church-narcissism embodies the false principle: "The church was not made for man but man for the church."

This is simply institutionalism. "This self-centered church cannot possibly administer effectively to the daily living and to the souls of its people," one layman asserts. "How can it show a mother how to perform a Christian ministry to her children, husband, and neighbors?" Rather it aims at swallowing up her energies in its various programs. And how can it show a man his Christian duties in his "secular" career? What it does is "to tell him that all this is irrelevant to his religious life, and that he serves God only to the extent to which he surrenders time and energy to organized church activity."[1]

Eberhard Mueller, director of the Evangelical Academy at Bad Boll in Germany, has suggested that the devil is pleased to have Christians concentrate on parish activities while the devil himself possesses the common life and controls the vast superstructures of modern society. This he terms the Babylonian Captivity of the church in the parishes.

The truth is that a ghettoed, introverted church not only fails her laymen but also fails the world around her. And she misses her own purpose, namely, "to serve the present age." She does not fulfill her calling.

E. Stanley Jones, famous American missionary-evangelist, once told about a fort in India which had been erected by the Colonial Army early in the British era. It stood upon a hill in the center of the strategic town of Jaipur in order to protect its inhabitants from marauders. As many years passed, the fort rigidly observed its rituals of garrison life—flag ceremonies, gunfire at sunset, spit-and-polish drill routines. Slowly, almost imperceptibly the town moved away from that hill toward a center of commerce nearby. One day the town was attacked and destroyed before troops from the fort could reach it.[2]

[1] *The Lutheran*, March 7, 1956, pp. 17–18.
[2] This story is told by Bruce Weaver in *The Lutheran*, January 24, 1962, p. 12.

In a world that is rapidly changing, the church has continued to live in the ways of an earlier, slower-moving age. As it seeks to perfect its rituals and to solve its internal problems it has allowed its basic responsibilities to slip from its effective reach.

The unhappy divorce between society and church means sterility for both of them. Eberhard Mueller has compared this separation between the world and the Christian fellowship to a dry garden with dusty, cracked earth lying alongside a stagnant stream of water without the irrigation channels that could mean life for both of them.

The Task: To Turn Around

The only solution to this predicament lies in moving the church into the common life of men, into politics and economics, into the daily round of work and play. One sentence which came out of the Evanston Assembly of the World Council of Churches has been echoed repeatedly, simply because it is so true: "The real battles of the faith today," Evanston declared, "are being fought in factories, shops, offices and farms, in political parties and government agencies, in countless homes, in the press, radio and television, in the relationship of nations." In 1961 at the New Delhi Assembly delegates asserted that "the outgoing church, rather than the ingrowing one, is likely to learn what the common life in Christ really is." If the Gospel is to live in today's world, it will do so only as the church faces whole men in their whole need in their whole web of human relations. Olov Hartman, director of the lay center at Sigtuna in Sweden, claims that "the high vault of the church extends over all the problems of the nation and of society."

High above the Mersey River in Liverpool stands St. Nicholas Church. Ships carry the city's commerce on the river, and in the market place at the river's edge these cargoes are distributed to meet the needs of the populace. From its lofty position the church used to turn its back upon these centers of human barter and toil. It seemed to beckon those who entered to direct their gaze to a distant altar shrouded in gloom.

But the church has been shattered by bombs. Now, in the framework of its ruins, a hut of modern design has appeared. *It is facing the other way.* The former porch is the present chancel, and its backdrop is a sharp-etched view of market place and river commerce.

Here, says George MacLeod, is a parable for the modern church. It must turn around and face the common life of men. Instead of trying to draw men away from this world into a quiet sanctuary, the church must carry Christ's broken body into market place and thronging traffic. "I simply argue," MacLeod insists, "that the Cross be raised again at the centre of the market-place as well as on the steeple of the church. I am recovering the claim that Jesus was not crucified in a cathedral between two candles, but on a cross between two thieves; on the town garbage-heap; at a crossroad . . ."

Christ died "at the kind of place where cynics talk smut, and thieves curse, and soldiers gamble." Besides, "that is what He died about." Obviously, MacLeod concludes, "that is where churchmen should be and what churchmen should be about."[3] Of course, it is laymen, rather than clergymen, who are most naturally found at the crossroads and those places where cynics and thieves gather. The dilemma of the split-apart layman and the gulf between pew and pavement are the same problem.

The urgency of the need for change is heightened by contrasting the present situation with the description of the

[3] *Only One Way Left* (Glasgow, Iona Community, 1956), p. 38.

church in the New Testament. In the following chapter several biblical illustrations of the meaning of the layman's participation in the church will provide a plumb line with which to measure the sag in contemporary church life.

CHAPTER III

BIBLICAL PICTURES OF THE LAITY

The Church Is People

If the man from Mars sticks his atomic disintegrator into your ribs and barks, "Take me to your church," what will you do? You could take him to a corner downtown and show him some buildings. But we know that is not the church and we wouldn't want Martians to become as confused as the earthlings are at this point. You could take him into the church office and give him the brochure announcing Lenten services or the annual report detailing the activities of the last year. But then the church is not religious activity any more than it is a building. The church is people, and not just people when they are participating in religious activities or when they belong to a religious organization.

It would be better to turn to the office wall and show him the map with the pins in it. This map would make it clearer that the church is people who are usually scattered throughout the community. But then this man from Mars might fall into the trap where so many Americans lie; he'd think that the church is people in two facets of life: when they are being religious and when they are involved with the family and home.

Now Luther and the Reformers took a giant step when they succeeded in telling people that they have Christian tasks as householders and family men. But home life is shrinking today and Christians should long since have realized that Luther meant to involve *all of life*. We wouldn't want to infect Mars with such limping and limited pictures of the church.

Probably the best thing to do when confronted on the street by this Martian is to look at your watch. If it is eight A.M., explain that most of the church is eating breakfast and it wouldn't be polite to visit the church at breakfast. If it is ten A.M., point out that most of the church is pretty busy and quite scattered in factories and offices and supermarkets and astride tractors. If it is Saturday afternoon, take him along to the ball game. Above all, tell him that since you are the church he can just as well watch you walk down the street!

There is real significance in insisting that the church is people. It is all those people who have faith in Jesus Christ. It is people in their total being—body and spirit, twenty-four hours of the day, seven days of the week, in every aspect of human experience, scattered into any and every place.

In the New Testament, more than eighty analogies are used to describe these people who are the church. In this chapter three of the major analogies will he held up as a contrast to the situation of the layman in today's church.

The author of I Peter, building upon a passage in Exodus (19:1–6), states the core of the matter succinctly: "But you are a chosen race, a royal priesthood, a holy nation, God's own people, that you may declare the wonderful deeds of him who called you out of darkness into his marvelous light. Once you were no people but now you are God's people" (2:9–10).

A Called People of God

Christians are not only people, they are *a* people. That is to say, they are a community like a race or a nation. In fact, they are an organism and each Christian belongs in an integral way—like limbs as parts of a tree, or the hands and eyes and other organs which make up the human body. Christians are the Body of Christ, Paul declares, and members of one another (I Cor. 12:27, Eph. 4:25).

God has done this. Christians are his chosen race, his special people. "Once you were no people but now you are God's people." Like a traveling troupe of actors who have been thrust together to live as a unit and to act as a single company at the director's behest, Christians have been called by the director of history into a community that is to participate together in the drama of human events.

God's purposes are thus served. The Christian calling is a summons from the supreme authority into a team that is a task force for carrying out his purposes.

It started in the Old Testament when God summoned a nation, Israel, to be his people and to fulfill his purpose of healing for all nations. Later, after many defections and rescues, the emphasis shifts to a remnant of Israel that will function as God's people and purpose for the nations.

In the New Testament Christ Jesus is that remnant. He answers the summons. In one sense he perfectly fulfills the purpose of God. In another sense he only initiates the fulfillment of that purpose and thus becomes the head of a new race or people to whom the summons comes. The New Testament calls God's people the *ecclesia*, those who are called out or summoned or assembled.

Ambassadors for Christ

What is the purpose of the church? Why has God summoned Christians? ". . . that you may declare the wonderful deeds of him who called you out of darkness into his marvelous light." "To serve the present age, My calling to fulfill." In II Corinthians (5:20) Paul asserts ". . . we are ambassadors for Christ, God making his appeal through us." Here is a really helpful picture—the church as an embassy and Christians as ambassadors.

But the word ambassador must be explained, lest one imagine a political big shot enjoying a political plum as a temporary representative of one powerful nation in the middle of the social affairs and diplomatic intrigue of a foreign capital. An ambassador is supposed to be the man with the mission of representing his country in another nation.

The church is God's mission and churchmen are God's apostles. *Envoys* is the right word. Christians are dispatched upon a mission in God's behalf. Christ is God's Apostle (Heb. 3:1). Christ's church carries that apostolate: "As the Father has sent me, even so I send you" (John 20:21). Not only does the church have a mission, but she *is* mission. She exists by mission just as fire exists by burning. Christians are naturally those who give away the Gospel. The good news of Jesus Christ is like a flowing mountain stream. It cannot be caught in a cup and labeled "mountain stream." Its receiver can be only a channel or pipe through which it takes its course to others.

As envoys Christians have citizenship in heaven (Phil. 3:20), but they are assigned to live in this world. They dwell in an alien land as representatives of the Kingdom of God and bearers of the good news, God's Word, from that kingdom. Churchmen are not "of" this world but are "sent into" this world as Christ's envoys, through whom God makes his appeal. This very idea was put in a different image by the New Delhi Assembly of the World Council of Churches: "We Christian people, wherever we are, are a letter from Christ to His world." (See II Cor. 3:3.)

But these ambassadors do not remain aliens. They identify with the people to whom they go. They take up citizenship in this other land. Today some foreign missionaries—if they go, for example, from the United States to India—are going to have to take citizenship in their adopted land or they will not be acceptable there. That is an analogy for the whole existence of the modern church. Christians take up a dual citizenship. They not only are "sent into" the world but also exist "for" the world. Ordinary ambassadors might not so identify themselves with the nation to which they go. Christians do identify themselves with this whole world. Christ does. He died for all of it and he is Lord of it all. "For God so loved the *world* that he gave his only Son . . ." (John 3:16). "God was in Christ reconciling the *world* to himself" (II Cor. 5:19). The church's purpose is fulfilled when she identifies with the world because she is the incarnation of God's saving purpose for the world.

As H. H. Walz puts it:

I rather think that from the very beginning Church and world are related to one another in such a way that theologically speaking neither could exist without the other. They have their very nature not in themselves but in their relationship. The history of the Church is the history of God's saving purpose and this purpose would really be purposeless if it were not directed toward the world.[1]

God's embassy, then, consists of envoys for Christ whose purpose causes them to identify with the world.

Royal Priests for the World

No embassy, however, belongs to the land where it is found as thoroughly as Christians belong to this world. Not only are they identified with the world; they are part of it. The church is made up of human beings. While they are called by God to be his people, they remain human beings and very much a part of the world. As Christians they con-

[1] *Laymen's Work,* Spring 1955, p. 7.

tinue to be creatures within the whole natural creation and men who belong to a common humanity. There can be no split between the true church and the real world. Furthermore, even though Christians are called out of commitment to sin and self and Satan, they remain sinners enmeshed in the web of evil and rebellion against God which entangles the whole human race. For these reasons, it is necessary to add to the idea of ambassadors, coming from another realm, the idea of priests, who emerge from among the people they serve.

Christians are "a royal priesthood" for the world. The role of a priest is twofold. He stands in the world for God, obeying him and proclaiming his mighty deeds. Calling the church an embassy expresses this role. He also stands before God for the world, carrying the world's adoration and intercession. Calling the church a royal priesthood expresses this role. Christians are those set apart within the world to represent all mankind before God. Christians are the part for the whole, a representation of all mankind, the elect who come forward for the totality.

A member of the second-century church expressed this idea well (in *Letter to Diognetus*), picturing Christians as the soul within the body of the world:

Christians cannot be distinguished from the rest of the human race by country or language or customs. They do not live in cities of their own; they do not use a peculiar form of speech; they do not follow an eccentric manner of life . . .

Yet, although they live in Greek and barbarian cities alike, as each man's lot has been cast, and follow the customs of the country in clothing and food and other matters of daily living, at the same time they give proof of the remarkable and admittedly extraordinary constitution of their commonwealth. They live in their own countries, but as aliens. They have a share in everything as citizens, and endure everything as foreigners. Every

foreign land is their father land, and yet for them every father
land is a foreign land . . .

They busy themselves on earth, but their citizenship is in
heaven . . .

To put it simply: What the soul is in the body, the Christians
are in the world.[2]

In fairness it should be pointed out that this ancient author
is not simply emphasizing that Christians belong to and
serve the world. He is stressing that Christians, who do belong and serve, are *called and committed to God within
the world*. Thus he adds: "The soul dwells in the body,
but does not belong to the body, and Christians dwell in
the world but do not belong to the world." Christians belong in every way except in final commitment—but that
changes the meaning of all belonging. They are a peculiar
people, a "new race." They both belong and do not belong.
They are both priests and ambassadors, God's special people.

Clearly this royal priesthood is one ministry and is in behalf of the whole world. The passage in I Peter makes that
evident: "But you are . . . a royal priesthood . . . that you
may declare the wonderful deeds of him who called you
out of darkness into his marvelous light." The priest relates
men and human activity to God. Only Christ, the one High
Priest, can actually do that, but he does it through the
church. Thus the church as priest relates mankind and the
whole earthly enterprise to God.

Now, however, to say that the church is a royal priesthood
not only helps to describe the churchman's relationship to
the world but also says something significant about the
church's own make-up. She is one kingly body. Whatever
the differences among Christians in their priesthood, it
cannot be argued that some have a kingly role and others a

[2] *Early Christian Fathers* (Philadelphia, Westminster, 1953) ed. and
trans. C. C. Richardson, pp. 216–18, quoted in *Laity*, November 1957, p. 7.

lesser, menial role. The whole church has a royal priesthood.

Furthermore, *all* Christians participate in this priesthood. *Every* Christian has a ministry in and for the world. Baptism means entrance into the church. It also means ordination into her ministry. At baptism each Christian is commissioned into the army of ambassadors and priests. The word "sacrament" came originally from the military oath taken when one joined the ancient Roman army. The sacrament of baptism involves the oath of participation in the task force of the church.

Even more important, this sacrament is an act of God and bestows upon the new member the gifts of the Holy Spirit. These gifts are not only forgiveness and salvation but also the gifts of a minister, those necessary for the church's mission. Every Christian is given a measure of such gifts of the spirit, though there is great diversity in their expression: "there are varieties of gifts, but the same Spirit" (I Cor. 12:4).

Some among the baptized may be given gifts which function more readily within the Christian home—infants, for example. Others may be so gifted as to serve best within the organized congregation's life—clergymen, for example. Infants and clergymen do belong to the royal priesthood. They do have a ministry for the world, but somewhat limited—infants because of limited human resources and clergymen because much of their work lies within the priesthood itself, ministering to laymen ministers.

Laity and Clergy

Now it becomes necessary to distinguish between laymen and clergymen, even though this chapter has stressed that the church is by nature one—a unity in mission, a called people. The Greek word for "people" in I Peter is *laos*, which is the word from which our term "layman" comes.

Originally the laity of God meant all Christian people, including clergymen. It is this whole laity which is Christ's embassy and the world's priesthood. But to refer to baptism as ordination and to speak of a variety of ministering gifts raises the question of the role of the ordained clergy, the set-apart ministry within the total royal priesthood.

Clergymen are and do for the church herself what laymen are and do for the world. The distinction is important, but it is a difference of function and emphasis only. Within the total priesthood some exercise their gifts and spend their time and energies largely among fellow Christians. Others (the nonclergy Christians) exercise gifts and spend themselves primarily in relation to the rest of the world. Clergymen, then, are those who first of all minister to laymen ministers.

Traditionally three roles have distinguished the clergyman. From the perspectives of this chapter each finds its meaning recast. For one thing, he is responsible for soul care, a pastor-counselor. Within the royal priesthood this means that he will minister to priests, serve the servants, counsel to help laymen fulfill their services, patch up the soldiers so that they will be able to resume their work on the battle lines. He will also cultivate and co-ordinate the gifts within the congregation's life that there be harmony within the fellowship and an effective witness to the world.

A second traditional function is that of the teacher. In this role the clergyman now becomes the resource man, the one trained in the skills and the traditions, who can therefore discover the ministering gifts which laymen have, train those gifts, and help point toward their use, whether within or beyond the royal priesthood itself.

Both these functions (soul care and teaching) could take their focus from Ephesians 4:11-12, which probably should read like this: "[Christ's] gifts were that some should be apostles, some prophets, some evangelists, some pastors and teachers [all these are clergy], *for the equipment of the saints for the work of ministry,* for building up the body of Christ." Such a reading eliminates the comma after "saints" and makes it clear that clergy, far from being "the ministry," equip the other saints for their ministry. That is, clergy are given offices within the church's organization for the purpose of building up or equipping all Christians for their mission to the world.

This can be put another way in connection with a third traditional function of clergymen. They conduct corporate worship, preach the Word and administer the sacraments. This means that they preach the Word at the center of the organized Christian community, whereas laymen proclaim that Word and are its demonstrators at the borders of the community and out in the world.

Laymen—to repeat—are and do for the world what clergy-men are and do for the church. Clergy work chiefly where the Word is recognized and Christ's Lordship acknowledged. Laymen work chiefly where these are not explicitly known. Clergy work with things *directly* identified with God, lay-men with things *indirectly* identified with God. Clergy work largely where the Gospel is openly acknowledged. Laymen work in the secular spheres where some autonomy must prevail. Laymen deal with things that are transient and rel-ative. Laymen priests relate transient, secular things to God. The merchant, the machinist, and the mayor are God's ministers, and their places of witness are the market place, the shop and the city hall.

Where are the laymen fulfilling such a ministry-in-the-world? Of course, they are not easily discovered, since each is quietly at work in his own sphere of daily activity. Yet any acute observer of the contemporary scene will conclude that such people are rare birds. It is the purpose of this volume to describe the ministry of this scarce, scattered, and hidden species and to call for its increase.

His Way of Life

CHAPTER IV

RHYTHM IN THE LAYMAN'S WEEK

If God is on the second floor and mankind as a whole is on the first floor, the church should be running the stairs between (to use a homely illustration). Actually, too many Christians and much too much of the church's organized life remain on the staircase landing—out of touch, knowing God only as footsteps above and knowing human need only as so much sweat and outcry below. What is badly needed is that Christians shall constantly be moving up to God, thrusting themselves more profoundly into their Christian resources of Bible study, prayer, sacraments, spiritual retreat, and discipline. And *at the same time* they should be hurrying down with healing for all the open sores to be found along man's daily concourse and for all the hidden abscesses in human hearts and minds.

The church's life is a rhythm or dialectic. Its members go up and come down, move in and then out, retreat and attack, withdraw only to penetrate the world once more. One's picture of the church should draw it as stretched thin between God's Word and the world, showing it as people moving in alternation between the cross and human need.

In the House of the Interpreter at the Five Oaks conference center at Paris, Ontario, the chapel lectern presents three niches facing the worshiper. In the center one is a large piece of rock salt. In the niche above stands a wooden cross. Below these lies a small globe of the world. There is no better way to interpret the church than to picture salty people living between the cross—source of saltness—and the world as the place where that salt spends itself usefully.

Of course such pictures have their limitations. Instead of rock salt, Christians should be salt in solution and in flowing motion, dispersing into their many places of service. And it is surely wrong to think of God on one floor and mankind on another. God is down there with his creatures more fully than any Christian can be. After all, he makes them and upholds them all at every moment. In fact, "the nearer the Church draws to its Lord the nearer it draws to the world." Nonetheless, the rhythmic motion remains as a crucial feature of the Christian life.

Two Phases

The point here is that the church exists always in *two phases*. Its constant rhythm is one of *Assembly* and *Dispersion*, just as Christ alternatingly urged his followers, "Come unto me" and "go into all the world" (Matt. 28:19, John 17:18). Only a filmstrip could adequately show the church as assembling and dispersing and assembling again unceasingly. We assemble in order to worship, study the Bible, pray, and have intense Christian fellowship. We disperse into our many places in the world in order to serve, to do our work, and to fellowship with these other people.

The previous chapter pointed to a duality in the church's life by distinguishing between clergy leadership in corporate worship within the church's organization and a lay leadership in ministry within the world. The real duality is not between clergymen and laymen but between two phases in the church life of any Christian. He assembles with fellow Christians, and then he goes out into his own particular place and activities in the rest of the world. It is just that the clergyman, who is professionally involved in the assembled phase, in the church's organization and the needs of the Christians themselves, does not ordinarily have as much time and energy and gifts to bestow on the remainder of the human panorama. There is always danger, of course, that the most committed laymen will become so clericalized and domesticated within parish activities that they will fail to give themselves to the rest of their world.

These phases—Assembly and Dispersion—are equally essential to the church. In neither is the church more the church than in the other, though its members spend more time dispersed than assembled. Neither phase *is* the church without the other. Sometimes we misunderstand that Greek word *ecclesia*, the New Testament word for church which means *called out*. We may think we are called by God out of the world to worship on Sunday morning and thus become the church. Not so! We are called out of allegiance to worldly things, from being "worldly," into the Kingdom of Heaven. We become a peculiar people, but entirely within this world, people of a special condition within an ordinary place. We are just as "called out," just as "gathered" in the theological sense when we are dispersed as when we assemble to worship. These two phases must remain balanced in importance or the church's true rhythm will be jarred.

In a significant sense worship, and all the *assembled* activity, is *preparation* for dispersion, for our service in the world, for the layman's ministry *out there*. Especially is this true of that congregational activity which is not corporate worship. This is all strictly instrumental, and not instrumental to the organizational growth primarily, but as preparation for the Christian's ministry outside. On Sunday we pause from our real church work to refresh and prepare for another week of being churchmen in the world. Worship is the springboard which we touch for a moment in order to be thrown back into the choppy waters of the daily routine. An apt legend over the exit from the nave of a church in Flushing, New York, reminds the departing worshiper, "As my Father hath sent me, even so send I you." "The holiest moment in the service of worship," declares Paul Van Buren, "is the moment when the Church gets up and goes out of the doors of the church building into the world."

In one of Ezekiel's visions (chapter 47) he is shown the temple with water rising near the altar and flowing right out through the main doorway. As he follows its flow it becomes a mighty stream in the desert, bringing new life everywhere, even making fresh the stagnant waters of the sea. Our assembled worship is surely our place of mighty resource to make us living waters poured out upon dusty, parched earth and stagnant pools.

Our assembled, corporate worship is, so to speak, rehearsal. Here on Sunday at eleven we worship God in practice session *among ourselves* in order that we may more skillfully worship him the rest of the week scattered among other people. Liturgy has been called the family activity of the church. Here we adore God and intercede for the world before him encouraged and guided and inspired by our fellow Christians. The rest of the week it is our ministry, as the people of God, to adore him and intercede for the world *in the midst of the world.*

Worship as a Sign

But now our corporate worship is not only preparation for the lay ministry in the world. It is also a part of that ministry. It is a sign. Our assembly before God is meant to be a sign to the world. After all, God speaks to the world in signs. The angels said to the shepherds, "This will be a sign for you: you will find a babe wrapped in swaddling clothes . . ."

Not only was Christ's coming a sign, but his words were signs (parables) and he performed startling acts of healing that were signs. There is theological reason for one to use pictures in describing Christ's body, the church, and in pointing to the lay ministry.

Similarly our worship is a sign. Preaching is a rather foolish one in a world in which people are always warning their friends, "Don't preach at me." Yet God uses preaching to speak his Word. Sacraments are signs pointing to Christ. Of course, they may seem like only a touching ceremony for babies, a sociable gathering at the front of a church, a bit of hocus-pocus (that very word comes from the derision poked at the Mass in the Middle Ages).

In fact, that's the trouble with corporate worship in our day: it utterly fails to be a convincing sign to unbelievers. Our preachments carry no authority; modern man is flooded with words that are too often cheap and deceptive, so that he no longer listens. Our sacraments don't point to the unseen Presence. Our solemn assemblies no longer startle anybody. In the Sermon on the Mount Christians are called "a city set on a hill" which "cannot be hid." But no one is looking at us any more when we dress up on Sunday and parade into the building and sing our hymns. If someone does look, he is likely to think it is just a parade of self-righteous hypocrites. Or he dismisses it as fraternal pageantry or playing at medieval knighthood.

Do not misunderstand. These signs remain meaningful within the Christian company. They are channels of grace for us. Preaching and sacraments are the true marks of the church, as the sixteenth-century Reformers insisted. If you want to find the true Gospel and true fellowship of believers amid a corrupt church organization, as Luther did, look for Gospel preaching and sacraments. These are the inner marks, the signs that are precious to believers.

Outer Marks Needed

But today we must find outer marks, signs that attract unbelievers, because now the church lives in a missionary situation in a sense not true for the Reformers. Everywhere in the world today the company of Christians is a minority surrounded by pagans or people indifferent to Christ. This may not be obvious in the United States, but it is quite true here too. Over the centuries those churches which stem from the conservative Reformation (inspired by Luther and Calvin) have failed in this matter in a significant way.

They have not properly emphasized the church's purpose. This shortcoming is illustrated in the Augsburg Confession, by which Lutherans define the church as "the congregation (or fellowship) of saints, in which the Gospel is rightly taught (or preached) and the Sacraments are rightly administered." This is a valuable definition and an admirable confession against the Roman Church of 1530. But it does not make clear that the church's purpose is to proclaim the Word of God *to the world*.

Succeeding generations of Protestants have allowed their image of the church to become quite narrow, seeing primarily people assembled on Sunday morning at eleven to listen to preaching and to receive sacraments. Laymen have come to think of their part in this church as showing up on Sunday and passively receiving blessings. They have lost any sense of being ambassadors or priests outside the assembly during the remainder of the week.

The church is a fellowship, all right, but a *proclamatory* fellowship. It gathers about the Word, but it is at its best when all proclaim the Word to the world, not when one preaches and other believers listen. We must all hear the Word repeatedly. And some few are set apart to preach sermons. But we all, the whole People of God, are set apart to proclaim the Word to the world. Obviously this involves not simply words on Sunday but a lifetime of being and doing and speaking. William Gowland has suggested that Paul's question (Rom. 10:14) "And how are they to hear without a preacher?" is a challenge not to the preacher on a Sunday to give a better sermon but to the layman "to become an interpreter in his varied contacts in the life of the world."

Our definition of the church ought to describe it as a fellowship of believers who assemble and then disperse, moving out from preaching and sacraments to carry the Word to the world. The church must be a catapult that hurls Christ-bearers into every distant corner of human society.

The Reformation raised as one of its great battle cries this phrase: the priesthood of all believers. This meant that each Christian is his own priest, standing directly before God without an intermediary. And it also meant that the church is a mutal ministry—each Christian caring for his fellow churchmen. Today we must add that this priesthood is the whole church as one royal priesthood functioning in behalf of the whole human race.

Besides, conservative Protestantism has not adequately shifted its stance to face into the twentieth century. Sixteenth-century beginnings were made within a corrupted Christian society called Christendom. For more than a century Protestants were forced to be defensive, preserving the purity of their worship and faith against relentless adversaries. Thus they focused upon the inner marks of preaching and sacrament.

But in the twentieth century Christendom has disappeared. There is no culture or geographic territory that can be so labeled as Christian. Everywhere in the world today Christians find themselves in the middle of secular and pagan cultures, rubbing elbows with people who are indifferent or hostile to Christ. We are called upon to witness to out-

siders. To the inner marks there must be added the outer
marks of a missionary church. It may be that in East Germany, where an enemy totalitarian state presses with increasing harshness, pure worship is a real witness to
unbelievers. In America it will require other signs to be
effective agents of the Gospel.

Luther claimed that the church "is outwardly known by
the holy possession of the Holy Cross." Today it is clear
that a witnessing church must evidence itself to unbelievers
in the marks of outgoing love and sacrificing service. Later
chapters will develop this theme.

Bruce Weaver, Washington clergyman, draws a modern
parable by comparing the institutional church to the amaz-
ingly large, complex, and expensive launching pads at Cape
Canaveral. This vast installation on the coast of Florida is
sheer waste unless those pads actually serve their purpose
of launching rockets into space. The organized church is
also a massive installation. It too is so much waste unless
it launches the people of God "into orbit among the complex
and sometimes dangerous constellations of human relationships such as politics, industry, the professions, education,
domestic life."

The true church has a rhythmic alternation in its life—
withdrawal and engagement, worship and scattered witness.
If the church loses either phase, its pulsations are inter-
rupted so that both worship and witness suffer. This fact is
stressed in the following story mime, which was acted out
at a conference on lay training held in Switzerland.[1]

In the first scene a workman comes to a complicated
machine in order to set it going. As he works on it he finds
himself more and more dominated by it. Then he himself
becomes a machine, no longer a human being.

The second scene takes us into a church. A Christian

[1] The story mime of the next four paragraphs is taken (altered) from
Laity, June 1956, p. 22.

comes to worship. He remains in the church and gradually becomes a lifeless part of the church building and loses all human contact.

In the third scene we see the empty church and, scattered outside, some people at their daily work. After a while they enter the church to worship and after the service return again to their respective occupations. This repeatedly acted rhythm of gathering and scattering, of worship and work, Sunday and weekday, shows the real life of a Christian community.

The last scene begins where the first and the second ended: we see the man-turned-machine in the plant and the lifeless worshiper in the church. But now the Christian community appears: after the gathering in the church, a member of the community remains and delivers the lifeless Christian from his estrangement and leads him back into the world. And now that the community is scattered again, a member becomes aware of the man enslaved by the machine. He remains with him, works with him, and helps him to free himself from the domination of the machine.

CHAPTER V

DIMENSION IN THE CHRISTIAN LIFE

As the church moves to its outgoing phase, namely, scattered among all the walks of life and into every weekday activity, laymen take up their central ministry. They become the church in the world. In fact, that is the definition of laymen being used in this volume—those whose primary witness comes while they are dispersed in the world, as distinguished from those whose main responsibilities lie within the organized church itself.

This means that the world can be defined as the habitat of laymen, all of God's creation aside from the church itself. The world is the public square within which the Christian is called upon to be a representative of Christ. It is those activities and events which make up the daily routine. It is those other people who throng this whole earth and especially those who make up our weekday associations.

We live in a day when great religions struggle for the total allegiance of men—Communism, Islam, Buddhism, Christianity. But the arena of struggle is not religion itself; it is the common life amid secular things—politics, recreation, economics, the workaday world of factories, gas stations, offices, farms, and hospitals. Laymen enter that arena regularly. They have a certain visibility: that is, as men they make some impact through the senses and through common-sense experiences. And they act in certain ways. But what is their peculiar quality that makes them signs of Christ before men? Paul claimed that he carried in his body the marks of Jesus; what stripes or wounds or marks do we bear?

Let us return to the illustration of the church as a traveling troupe of actors. Let us imagine that upon arrival at a given city the members scatter to enter into many different dramas with other casts. Each Christian is called into a particular stage which is his part of the world. He is given certain fellow actors, settings, and events. These too are his world. God has created all these. God is also the author of each play, and he is the audience in every case. There are no set scripts, only the promptings of the Holy Spirit and the occasional rehearsals with fellow Christians. It is the layman's ministry so to act as to show what God has done in Christ, so to enter into his own part that the other actors will sense the plot that underlies each production and the whole human drama.

First of All to Be

But here a warning must be sounded. It would be misleading to focus too readily upon being signs or bearing marks or playing a role. The Christian's ministry in the world does not primarily set him in search of a program, or projecting some self-conscious activities, or seeking the right sales pitch. It will not do to say "if only men will learn to speak up for Christ." This is not a matter of words, first of all, or of efforts, or even of intention, but of *dimension*, that special quality that is embedded in a peculiar people. We must first learn to *be* the church, the People of God in the world. Just as natural as breathing and walking, it should be our unconscious assumption that we are the church at all times. As actors on the world's stage Christians can only interpret what they authentically are within and can only unveil a plot which they honestly experience. If they *are* the church, then this fact will find expression in certain attitudes and actions and habits—a style of life. It will become quietly manifest to their neighbors that they are prompted by a different spirit, the Holy Spirit.

In the first centuries after Christ the church spread throughout the Roman Empire and became unobtrusively influential by a kind of quiet contagion. The earliest Christians were a spontaneously missionary church. After the apostles, one does not hear of any outstanding preachers or famous professional evangelists for several centuries. Humble and ordinary Christians carried an infectious spirit with them in all their daily contacts. The Gospel was carried along the trade routes by merchants and sailors. Domestic servants taught Christ in and through their domestic tasks; small shopkeepers did so through their trading. Wives won their husbands over to the faith by silent example (I Peter 3:1). Many anonymous laymen carried out their daily tasks as a Christian ministry, and the empire was finally conquered. This expansion took place not by words, nor by planned activities, but by lives that unconsciously evidenced a new, Spirit-filled dimension.

Today if the Christian message is to be received in America and among the other people of the far-flung world mission, it will be heard that way. Natives who are converted to Christ will continue to live in their former world and the missionaries will trust the Holy Spirit to work through them.

In the past century it has not been that way. Usually missionaries have gone into a foreign land and bought property to build a compound with a church and school and hospital and industrial plant. Then they have proceeded to bring their converts into the sheltered compound, away from their former associations.

Roland Allen, an early-twentieth-century prophet, attacked this method. He claimed that the compound and its institutions created a new caste or a ghetto. Its visibility and activity blocked the spontaneous witness of Christians dispersed in the world. "When men see a change in the lives of their neighbors," Allen asserted,

who have previously lived a life in all respects identical with their own, and whose life is still in nearly all its outward aspects identical with their own; when they see such neighbors changed, doing the same things that they do themselves but doing them with a difference, in a different spirit; when they see them united in a church, which is a living body in the place, and in which the Spirit resides which appears to affect the conduct of its individual members; then they inevitably begin to wonder and to question the cause . . .[1]

In this way outsiders are confronted by the Holy Spirit. Of course the foreign missionary cannot observe this and is tempted to enlist the convinced native in a school or preaching band, which soon overshadows the little, everyday acts and events of a lay witness. Thus the institution thwarts the spontaneous expansion of the church because it is hard to trust the unseen power of the Holy Spirit. Similarly in America denominational executives and clergymen build up the organization, recording progress in statistics, and in this manner often block the unseen and unheard witness of neighbor to neighbor in the community.

Bishop Lesslie Newbigin tells of his frequent experience upon visiting a South Indian village. All the Christians join him in procession, followed by a curious crowd of other inhabitants of that village. At the church steps he turns, with the Christians seated nearest to him and the Hindus and Moslems standing in an outer circle. Here he preaches to the non-Christians before entering for Christian worship. "When I do that," he points out,

[1] Quoted in *Laity*, November 1957, p. 14.

I always know one thing: The words I speak will only carry weight if those who hear them can see that they are being proved true in the life of the congregation which sits in the middle.[2]

In an Indian village changed lives (or unchanged ones) will not remain hidden. Yet this graphic incident is a symbol not only for the church's witness in India but also for her effective outreach in any neighborhood or any setting. Only what the Christians actually are can give weight to the Gospel's claims. Only an infectious spirit abroad in the world through laymen can seem like genuine good news to outsiders.

Bernt Opsal, president of the Lutheran Bible Institute, relates the following incident, which took place on shipboard in the Far East when he was a Navy chaplain during the Korean conflict. One day Jim, one of the men who worked in the electrical shop, came in to see the chaplain.

"Chaplain, I can't stand it any longer," Jim said.

"What do you mean?" the chaplain asked.

"This guy Danny is just about impossible. In the shop we've been giving him a rough time because of his faith. We've been kidding him, riding him, and sometimes even being mean to him, but the more unkind we are, the nicer he is to us. On top of all this, he is very ready to help us out whenever we need someone to stand by and take on special assignments. He goes out of his way to be friendly and help out whenever he can. Besides that, he is the best electrician that we have in the shop. It has really bothered me.

"What's he got that I haven't got?" Jim asked intently.

Under such circumstances Chaplain Opsal was well able to tell Jim about Jesus Christ and to guide him into an active Christian faith.

[2] *The Lutheran*, April 5, 1961, p. 19.

The New Life

This emphasis—upon what Christians are—leads us back, of course, to the central understandings of the Christian faith. We live by God's grace through faith. We are no longer our own but belong to Christ. We are new creatures, St. Paul tells us (II Cor. 5:17). Since Christ is taking shape within us, we are being formed as new men after his image (Rom. 8:29, II Cor. 3:18, etc.). This is the dimension which Christians as God's peculiar people are to contribute to the world's need.

Paul gives several illustrations of what happens. It is like the slave who has been purchased or redeemed and given his freedom. It is like enemies who are reconciled and made friends. It is like a dead man made alive, given new life. It is like a stranger's being adopted and granted full sonship, like a debtor who is forgiven and freed of that weight, like a cutoff limb engrafted into a tree, like an unclean person washed and made clean again.

But if we view this new dimension from the standpoint of the layman's ministry in the world, at least four characteristics deserve mention: he is free, poised, integrated, alert.

Free

The peculiar dimension of the Christian means that he is *free* of selfishness and self-serving. Not completely, of course, since he still succumbs to sin. But he is not a slave to sin and selfishness any more because he knows he lives by resources beyond himself. The Christian is the one who has been taken care of by God in Jesus Christ. His salvation has been given him through his faith in Christ. The Gospel is good news, and that news is that God has forgiven the sinner and has accepted him, even though he still sins.

Here we are as human beings—all of us—creatures who rebel against God and try to make out on our own, trying to earn our salvation, to prove that we are good, straining to justify ourselves, trying to get ahead in an endless rat race, frantically stoking a furnace of pride, eagerly grasping at elusive success. We are self-servers, always intent upon taking care of number one. But God says: relax, trust Christ, hold on to him, just receive the good gifts of my grace in faith and you'll be taken care of. In ultimate matters—in eternal life and relation to God—you can stop worrying and striving.

This does not mean that the Christian's efforts are now crowned with success. Quite the contrary. His failures are now highlighted. When one receives God's grace he sees the futility of his own strivings, the deadly and inevitable sin that mars his every effort. He is moved to surrender and to look beyond himself for the good life. He is taken out of the struggle for success; he becomes able to live with his failures. For God has accepted him while he continues to be a sinner. Henceforth he lives by receiving and trusting God. Here is a working definition of faith. It is God's gift that brings a man a wholehearted trust in him. The man who has faith simply finds that he has been given the ability to be open to God's gifts, to receive them and to trust God. As he becomes bound to Christ he finds himself free of self-serving and ready for service to other people.

Not that the Christian always surrenders and always trusts when he faces his fellow men in daily work or ordinary associations. He works and sometimes he struggles and fights. But he knows that his salvation does not hinge upon his success. The desperation—the curse or the sting—is taken out of his hard work and frequent failures. This means he can serve God and his fellow men better. He is free to be unselfish because God has already taken care of him.

Poised

From such relaxed freedom comes a deep inner *poise* or balance. Because the Christian has God's grace as a free gift he is no longer anxious and insecure and unstable inside. He has poise and confidence. He does not always have to serve himself but is free to give full attention and energy to the demands made upon him.

Take the illustration of the ice skater. If he does not know how to skate, when he gets on his skates he will be wobbly and will grab his companion or any object to serve the purposes of his own balance. But if he has been taken care of, if he is eventually able to skate skillfully, he can consider his balance something that is given to him, to be taken for granted. He is able to give himself without thought for his own balance to the balance of his wobbly companion, to his part in the intricate procedures of the ice capades, or to participation in the contest in the hockey arena. God's grace in Christ gives us the balance, enabling us to be free to meet the demands made upon us.

Or we can use the boxer as an example. When he enters into the ring and makes decisions in a particular fight, he can consider his poise and his balance as given to him. He has worked and sweated for it in the past, but he does not think about the poise and the balance now. Rather he thinks about the stance and the footwork and can give himself to the situation and to concern about what his opponent is doing.

Such inner poise should make the Christian an able man within the chain of authority at the office or on the police force. If he lives by faith in God he will be responsive to his superior and will seek to please the boss without being over-anxious about that relationship. He will seek to serve the company and the public without always calculating personal advantage, without warping all actions toward securing personal favor or popularity or promotion. A policeman whose personality is one of relaxed good will can do much to set the tone of the whole neighborhood. The Christian policeman will not, in so far as he is a Christian, need to take out his frustrations on those who fall afoul of his authority. He will not blindly enforce rules without consideration for the humane and just act.

A recent television program pictured a rookie policeman who enforced a strange new ordinance, namely, no walking on the grass in the park. He acted without consideration of the circumstances and without any fairness. It was not a caricature of the policeman; rather, it showed a very rigid rookie who was rigid because he was insecure. The Christian can be flexible and fair because he is inwardly secure and relaxed. Incidentally, this is the stuff from which courage is made.

During World War II a conscientious objector named David was put in prison for his convictions. There his greatest hardship, he said, was the lack of privacy or opportunity for meditation. Yet he maintained an inner poise. One day a particularly cruel jailer kicked a crippled prisoner down a flight of stairs in the presence of a number of the inmates. Tempers flared, but David stepped forward with both calmness and vigor, quietly taking the jailer to task while averting violence. When David finally left the prison that jailer grudgingly admitted it was the first time he'd been sorry to see a prisoner leave.

In a Chicago meat-packing plant, where Negroes were being hired and various departments slowly desegregated, the gashouse of the plant had resisted. The white workers had scared away the first Negroes assigned there with simulated explosions and stories of violence. Then a more relaxed, bolder Negro—committed to the desegregation effort—took that assignment. The foreman tried to frighten him by taking him to the place where there were some small explosions. At other times workmen would act excited, as though about to flee a big explosion. But this Negro kept his head and decided he'd not run until others actually deserted the building. In a few weeks he was accepted and other Negroes were also taken into that department. Courage is like water in a tap: tenseness turns it off, relaxation turns it on.

When the author was a boy, he worked as a greenhorn on his uncle's farm. If rain threatened the hay crop, his efforts to hasten would grow frantic, losing their always slender effectiveness. Then his uncle, whose livelihood was involved and who could accurately judge the loss which wet hay brings, would chuckle, while working at top speed, "Oh well, it's all just for fun!"

That was not the carelessness of a man with no sense of responsibility. It was rather the nonchalance, the gay imperturbability, of one who lived by faith in God so that he could speak lightly amid the serious business of making a living. Many theologians mention genuine humor as a sign of Christian faith. "It is humor," says one theologian, "as opposed to the overseriousness of people who know only success and efficency, that makes secular things and human relations lighter." Even a king, if he is a wise one, keeps a court jester at his side to blow holes in the stifling air of sober pride. When one cannot take a good joke, his soul is wrapped too tightly in something other than God.

Integrated

However, the other side of the coin deserves mention too. The Christian who has been freed and given his balance also becomes responsible. He finds *integrity* or wholeness through his faith. Commitment to Christ brings a new inner consistency. Called by God, he has a singleness of purpose underlying his many tasks. He can be counted on as responsible.

He will put first things first among the myriad demands for
his attention. True, he still sins and he sometimes swerves
aside to serve himself. Yet he knows what his general direction must be, where to find wholeness. In Christ are
resources and real help in maintaining integrity.

Body and spirit find unity in Christ, letting up on their
struggle against each other. The Christian realizes that both
his body with its environing world of bodies, on the one
hand, and that radically different part, his spirit, with its
world of persons, on the other hand, are created by the same
God. He knows that God molds a given body and its spirit
into a unit, a man. Beyond this, the Christian knows that
he finds his completion in being integrated into a larger
universe whose unity consists of a common source, center,
and sovereign, namely, God. Here is true humility—the
ability to find one's place within the universe, neither over-
estimating nor underrating one's importance.

Conflicting duties have their place of appeal within the
Christian man also. The agony of decision is not removed,
but the Christian has a principle—his call to serve Christ—
by which he can judge among the various duties, responsibilities, and offices which fall upon him. His calls to be a
good parent, a willing citizen, an able workman, a wise
participant in his congregation—all are subsumed under one
call, and all can be given proper and balanced place within
a larger totality. He finds focus as a person when the priorities in his life fall into place.

Some few men find greatness in single-minded devotion
to a great task. Dag Hammarskjöld was one of these. As a
Swedish civil servant and then Secretary-General of the
United Nations he coupled an inner reserve with a complete
objectivity in all matters of politics, which made him a tal-
ented, devoted servant of world peace, patient under pressure, unruffled in crisis. He never married and formed few
warm friendships. He never propagandized or compromised

his strict neutrality even in questions of religion and philosophy so long as he was serving the United Nations with its motley gathering of peoples. At the dedication of the Meditation Room at the United Nations building in New York he spoke for a diversity of nations of all faiths when he said, "We all have within us a center of stillness surrounded by silence."

Yet for Dag Hammarskjöld himself, as a rare confession of faith makes clear, that stillness within was reserved for the God known in Jesus Christ. Influenced by Albert Schweitzer and the medieval mystics (on his last journey his only book was *The Imitation of Christ* by Thomas a Kempis), he combined the inner self-surrender and outer life of active social service which have characterized many of the Christian greats. He was a man of integrity who allowed the depth of his personal commitment to God to have the entire shaping of a life given in service to world peace.

The layman's dual citizenship remains. He is part of the Kingdom of God and at the same time committed to this-worldly pursuits. That's what it means to be a Christian layman. However, even as the tension mounts, the Christian trusts that there is an overarching unity, since God is in final control of both these worlds. And in the core of his person there is unity in Christ. He is given an inner consistency which can transform the layman's dilemma—split between church and world (see Chapter I)—into an alternating rhythm, a two-pronged way of meeting and serving the one God.

Alert

Equally important, the Christian is *alert*. An inner poise and integrity do not mean that he settles easily and stolidly into well-worn grooves. Habits play a large role within any person, but the Christian constantly steps aside to look at the ruts in his life. He seeks to reset his travel plan by breaking up old patterns to plot a new course. He keeps asking who he is and where he is going. He asks continually what Christ would have him do. He comes into a new self-awareness and self-criticism and finds his whole person probed and realigned by the one who has called him. Thereafter he sees all things in fresh perspective.

One of the executives in a large factory in southern Germany was feared by the men with whom he worked because he would ruthlessly talk them down in order to win his point. He attended some of the conferences at a Christian training center because, he said, he liked the frank discussion of deep problems. But here too he would answer someone else's opinion with a dogmatic twenty-minute speech and usually tried to summarize a discussion in order to tell those present what they should do. Finally a conference leader told him this was the wrong way to behave. He got angry. Yet he continued to return and obviously struggled with himself to limit his talking. Over a period of years his personality and way of dealing with people have undergone a marked change both in conferences and at daily work. He still has to struggle, but he imposes his opinions on others less frequently and has learned to listen with sensitivity to other viewpoints. He has become a more flexible and alert Christian personality.

This alertness and capacity for self-criticism is a gift of God. Men are largely creatures of habit and bound by the past except as God opens their eyes and puts them on tiptoe. But such awakening is both beginning and renewal of the Christian life. "You must be born again," whether suddenly or slowly, is an authentic and repeated element in Christian experience. When people met Jesus in the New Testament, we are frequently told, "their eyes were opened."

"He who has ears, let him hear" are words by which Jesus exhorted his listeners to a new awareness.

Beyond self-awareness, the Christian is continually re-sensitized to his whole environment. Especially does he become sensitive to the needs of other people, actually listening to their condition, really loving and compassionate toward them as unique persons. Harry DeWire asserts that "the tenets of love suggest that one's presence in the world should be *invitational and bidding*. The Christian is an 'open' person. He is aware of the subtle signs that indicate the degree of readiness which is basic for any relationship."[3] Everything human comes into the orbit of his concern. He becomes a man who is bound up fully with all humanity. "To be a Christian," as Robert Spike puts it,

is to be fully a man—a creature of God, not infallible, not isolated and sterilized by your religion, but responding as a whole being to the times and the people among whom one is set. It means further responding as one who has been freed by Jesus Christ to take a chance, to be experimental, to laugh at fate and cry with compassion, to work and to play: in short, to be a new creature, born of a new birth.[4]

Finally, being alert includes the ability to discern God at work in all the events and circumstances which life presents. The Christian sees the hand of God in the opportunities before him to help his neighbor in time of need. He seeks to find God's handiwork in all other happenings as well. Furthermore, he realizes that God is working, and calling Christians to be fellow workers, within the great contemporary issues in politics and economics. Even though the problems are of vast complexity and even though decisions seem to lie with powerful leaders, the Christian knows that he is responsible and must interpret and decide.

[3] *The Christian as Communicator* (Philadelphia, Westminster, 1961), p. 172.
[4] *To Be a Man* (New York, Association, 1961), p. 32.

A visiting German pastor and his American host became fast friends on a profound Christian level. Just as the pastor was leaving, he said, "I must ask you one question: What are you doing about atomic disarmament?" The American first felt guilt because he had pushed that issue from his mind. Then he felt irritation: "Oh no, not this again. How could I keep up with the details, and what difference would it make anyhow?" Then he faced up to it. Every American is deeply involved in this question. Every Christian American is called to be alert and keen in searching out God's will and action in the matter of atomic disarmament or in any other pressing social issue.[5]

The Christian will be free, poised, integrated, and alert. Of course, the peculiar quality of the Christian life could be described with other characteristics. Then, too, Christians fail frequently. They are not superior to other men. They often cut themselves off from their resources. Yet God has given them gifts which enable them to contribute through their lives a new dimension within the daily round. They can develop a responsible way of living that becomes a distinct style.

[5] This incident is related in a mimeographed sermon booklet, "A Christian Style of Life," by John S. Duley (Columbus, Ohio, 1959), p. 9.

CHAPTER VI

STYLE IN THE DAILY ROUND

Even though the People of God are a peculiar people, even though each one bears a new dimension and a new integrity within him, there will be no uniformity of actions and habits, no clear and all-inclusive pattern for the participation of Christians in the world about them. They will evidence in some measure the outward marks of a missionary church—a loving spirit and deeds of sacrificial service. But these will find no stereotype, no fixed and predictable pattern of reactions. Rightly understood, the church's life in the world can never harden into grooves or precise laws to which all members must conform.

Among Christians a distinct way of life does sometimes emerge. In fact, it is badly needed in America today. But such a style of life will be flexible, with many variations and frequent shifts. There are at least three reasons for this.

Three Reasons for Flexibility

For one thing, each human being is a unique creation of God with characteristics and potentialities exactly matched by no other human being. Sinning mars our distinctiveness until we often appear monotonously uniform. Paul Scherer labels sin as dull and lifeless, "a putrefying bit of gray carrion." When the Gospel redeems a man, it makes him fully human again, distinctly himself, the unique person God intended him to be. Clearly, it should be the Gospel-filled Christian who is refreshingly different, an interesting variation even from his fellow Christians.

Here is where the figure of Christ as the Good Shepherd finds some of its richest meaning. "I am the good shepherd," he tells us in the tenth chapter of John, adding that he knows his sheep (verse 14). This means that he knows them as individuals. The good shepherd "calls his own sheep by name and leads them out" (verse 3). Like the girl who minds the cows and names her charges, like the dog owner who names his pet—not just Bill or Bessie but names that fit the animal's looks or way of acting: Whitey, Baldy, Bushy, or Spot, and maybe Dopey and Bashful and Sneezy! The good shepherd respects their individuality. Sheep like calm water, but Dopey drinks only water that is perfectly still, so the shepherd finds it for him. Bashful is afraid of the narrow canyons, so the shepherd walks beside him in tight places, touching the frightened animal with his staff. "He leads me beside still waters. . . . Even though I walk through the valley of the shadow of death, I fear no evil; for thou art with me; thy rod and thy staff, they comfort me" (Ps. 23).

Just as Christ ministers to our individual needs, so we minister to others through our individual characteristics. Each of us reveals Christ to his neighbor in a unique manner, through his unique personality. Some years ago there appeared an unusual scene in the British Museum when the great sculptor Abraham Walkowitz was honored. Eleven of his friends sculptured Walkowitz's bust, but each pictured him as a different person, including some of that particular friend's own characteristics. This they did out of respect for Walkowitz's theory, namely, that an artist always gives some of his own characteristics to the subject he depicts. Well, each Christian's great work of art is to show forth Jesus Christ to those about him. And he puts some of himself into it, showing Christ through the personality and individuality of that particular disciple of the Master.

Therefore, in the same situation two men may react differently though they have the same commitment to Christ and the same desire to serve. Yet neither violates his own integrity. One may express a "holy impatience" which causes him to resist his boss's directive. The other may express a "holy patience" by trying to fulfill the questionable directive in a way that does not too greatly violate his conscience. One may be impelled to speak out openly against a politician's move, while the other quietly tries to change things within party circles. Some have a flair for provoking needed change. Others have a greater gift for patient waiting. Some Christians will with heavy hearts answer their nation's summons to warfare when the cause seems just or the conflict necessary. Others will find that the Gospel impels them to resist and become conscientious objectors. The same Gospel has a different consequence within different individuals. Sometimes, of course, disagreement means that our understanding is cloudy and our commitment tepid, but there is legitimate basis in God's creation itself for Christians to differ from each other at many points of specific action.

A second reason why no uniformity can emerge among Christians is that circumstances and situations differ radically. In the study of Christian ethics and in Bible study modern theologians are emphasizing that God's Word comes to men from beyond themselves "as the interpretation of a situation, requiring action in that situation." Each Christian must try to take the responsible and right action in his unique setting. Thus one man may resist his boss's directive and another seek to comply with his boss because the two bosses are quite different or because the boss-employee relationships are quite different. Probably the teacher has a better opportunity to exercise his conscience against the president of his school than the soldier or the policeman has against his superior officer. These are quite different situations.

In every instance the Christian must look carefully at the whole context, noting all the factors that bear upon the place of decision. Within all these influences and circumstances he looks for the hand of God at work and seeks to respond to God in his decision by fitting his own actions into God's actions. This means that he listens for the guidance of the Holy Spirit which is brought to him through his conscientious study of the situation. In this manner the making of Christian decisions is something of an art, free and creative, so that no two Christians will always respond in the same pattern.

In a recent discussion two Protestant nurses who worked in a Catholic hospital were complaining that they, along with everybody else, had to stop work when priests came by with the Host—bread and wine from Holy Communion, believed to be the body and blood of Christ—and had to bow before the Host. They felt that this violated their consciences and that they should disobey. But one theologian, who knew the intricate, interdependent teamwork of a large modern hospital, was quite sharp with them. "It is a life-and-death matter for nurses to obey and to obey completely; when you're on that hospital team you obey." He felt that their only alternative was to resign in such a situation.

On the other hand, anyone can get into a situation in which he should refuse obedience. Generally, Christian conscientious objection should be much more widespread than it is in our day. And this issue of obedience versus resistance is but one instance of the variations in the behavior that Christians will evidence.

It is, in the third place, primarily a matter of calling. We are called by God to be ourselves and to use our talents. We are called by God to serve Christ and our neighbor in the circumstances and situations that surround us in daily life. Not many of us are summoned as Abraham was to leave home dramatically for a pilgrimage into the unknown. Yet we are expected to respond, just as he did, in faithful obedience (Heb. 11:8), and we are expected to live "on call," summoned to a ministry in that part of the world that is given us as our setting. Albert Schweitzer felt that the Holy Spirit had called him to change his career into medical service in Africa. We are summoned to service, but most of us will likely answer the promptings of the Spirit in more routine ways in familiar places.

Even in familiar places we will respond in radically different ways. The English professor may show his students the recovery of the lost image of man within the novels of William Faulkner. The electrician may do his wiring with steady skill and honest effort. Each may fail to understand what the other is doing, yet each carries out a Christian calling. Upon graduation one Christian law student may take up a post on Wall Street with opportunity for rising influence. His classmate may bury himself in the problems and misery of Harlem humanity. It is possible that each thereby moves toward fulfillment of his calling in Christ.

W. H. Auden has pointed out how the encounter with Christ sends one man journeying and brings another home. When Wise Men and Shepherds come to the manger of the Christ child, the Wise Men say

> Led by the light of an unusual star,
> We hunted high and low. Have traveled far,
>
> . . . .
>
> By ruined arches and past modern shops,
> Counting the miles, And the absurd mistakes.
> Oh here and now our endless journey stops.

In contrast the Shepherds say

> We never left the place where we were born,
> Have only lived one day, but every day,
> Have walked a thousand miles yet only worn
> The grass between our work and home away.
>
> . . . .
>
> Tonight for the first time the prison gates
> Have opened. Music and sudden light
> Have interrupted our routine tonight,
> And swept the filth of habit from our hearts.
> Oh here and now our endless journey starts.[1]

Toward a Modern Style

Yet vital Christianity has usually found expression in a distinctive cut or style of living. This way of living has differed radically according to the age in which it emerges. No one can predict or himself produce the style for the coming decades in America. One can only safely predict that it will not be the same as that of any past generation. To copy any earlier age would mean reproducing an external pattern of conformity that expresses no inner integrity and carries through no mission to the contemporary world.

For example, the Amish and Mennonite "plain people," with their horse-drawn buggies and austere black clothes, have many admirable qualities, but their witness to the modern world is limited because their way of life speaks more loudly of quaint and curious habits belonging to the eighteenth century. In contrast some of the Quakers have tried to adapt to twentieth-century conditions without succumbing to the spirit of the age, with its conformism and compulsive violence. They continue to make their peace

---

[1] From "For the Time Being," from *The Collected Poetry of W. H. Auden* (New York, Random House, 1945), pp. 442–44, quoted in John A. Hutchison, ed., *Christian Faith and Social Action* (New York, Scribners, 1953), p. 114.

testimony through an American Friends Service Committee which serves both the cause of peace and modern human need in a wide-ranging, flexible program.

While Christianity has a hard core of meaning which does not change from age to age, many of its practices and habits are developed in response to a particular and passing phase of history. Certain Christian virtues will stand out according to the needs of a given age.[2] In a monastic age the ideal Christian will appear ascetic and innocent. In a Puritan age he will be thought of as vigorous, disciplined, and dutiful. In a romantic age the image is that of a courageous idealist who is both virile and chaste—exemplified in stories of the shining knights of King Arthur's Round Table.

John Bunyan's *Pilgrim's Progress*, which evoked a powerful response from many generations of Christians, cannot serve as our vision today. Its picture of a perilous journey to heaven through the many tempting pitfalls of life on this earth neither fits contemporary Christian thinking and experience nor has any power of attraction for other members of this secular generation. Its message of otherworldly withdrawal is not the needed note for our pilgrimage in the second half of the twentieth century.

The individual Christian's style of life will change over the decades. Those who are "followers of the Way" find that the terrain is new in each succeeding valley and mountain of the years. They will adapt to the features of the landscape without making it their home. They will accept the customs of the people where they now live, but they will not adopt their ways and purposes without alteration. In unconscious and unplanned ways there will grow up habits of daily existence which by common consent among Christians become signs of a distinctive inner commitment. If the inner commitment is a true and vigorous response to Christ and

[2] This point is made by Robert W. Spike in *To Be a Man*, p. 111.

the habits are attractive and outgoing, this style *may* present signs to unbelievers, appealing symbols of the faith. In the final analysis only God raises up convincing signs, but he can use the habits of Christian men and women to that end.

It has been suggested that Dietrich Bonhoeffer may emerge to be spokesman for a "holy worldliness" in the twentieth century as Bunyan spoke effectively for a "holy unworldliness" in bygone eras. Even as this young German theologian approached death at the hands of the Nazis at the end of World War II, he became more and more convinced that to be a Christian meant to be fully a man and to be thoroughly involved in the world's life and labor. For both Bunyan and Bonhoeffer the vision of a Christian style was wrought out amid persecution and in prison. Bunyan became a prophet calling Christians into a pilgrimage away from entanglement in the world's pursuits. Bonhoeffer in his *Letters and Papers from Prison* issues a prophetic call for modern Christians to immerse themselves in the problems and perils of the whole human scene. The "worldliness" of Christianity, he asserts, consists of

taking life in one's stride, with all its duties and problems, its successes and failures, its experiences and helplessness. It is in such a life that we throw ourselves utterly in the arms of God and participate in his sufferings in the world and watch with Christ in Gethsemane. . . . How can success make us arrogant or failure lead us astray, when we participate in the sufferings of God by living in this world?[3]

Not that we should emulate Bonhoeffer or carefully copy his ideas in order that we may make our mark as he has done. The process whereby we become signs is not a conscious procedure at all. Certainly it is neither a matter of

[3] This quotation is found in the American edition of this work, entitled *Prisoner for God* (New York, Macmillan, 1958), p. 169.

self-conscious imitation of a hero nor a self-conscious effort to be signs for other folk. We do not try to be joyful so that people around us will inquire and discover that Christ redeems. We do not rush to their help so that they will follow us to our Lord. We do not embrace martyrdom for the effect it will have. God alone raises up true signs. He uses saints who do not know they are saints. He uses Christians who are humble because they are not conscious of themselves. He uses a style of life which spontaneously takes shape between two poles—a savior, Jesus Christ, and people whose needs cry out.

In Conrad Richter's novel, *A Simple Honorable Man*, the central figure is a Lutheran clergyman at the turn of the past century who neglected his town parish in the coal regions of Pennsylvania in order to minister to the depressed people of Lost Run, a mountain coal town. Here, as Harry Donner tried to erect a little church and to help a mine-mangled parishioner, he had a run-in with the superintendent of the mine; but he continued to make friendly visits to the man's children.

One evening as he played and sang with the youngsters in their father's absence he smelled the unusually strong odor of carbide in the superintendent's house, but he did not sense the danger of an explosion, though the room was lighted by an open jet.

They were still singing and laughing when sudden steps sounded on the veranda and the front door opened. All was silent for a moment. Then with a strong oath the superintendent rushed in, threw the parlor windows wide, turned out the lights abruptly and left them in darkness. Presently they could hear him banging around in the cellar.

Harry Donner felt discomfited. He waited a little before standing up, said he guessed he had to go. He made a brief parting prayer in the darkness, uncertain whether any of the children were left in the room to hear him. Afterward he said good-by

and found his way to the door, grateful for the peace and star-
light outside. All the long road down the mountain that night he
pondered the happening, the strange behavior and the unheal-
able breach between him and the superintendent who went to
such lengths to oppose and eject him.

When Pastor Donner returned to Lost Run several days
later he found the whole village talking about how the
superintendent had returned home that night to find his
house full of escaping gas and had shut off the gas in the
cellar by flashlight. One of the women reported that the
superintendent had told his maid

"that he couldn't figure out how the house never blew up with
the lights turned on full in the parlor and the gas thick enough to
cut with a knife. He said there you all sat laughing and talking
as though nothing was the matter. He said the only thing that
saved his young ones was the presence of a good person in the
house."

"Which person did he mean?" Harry Donner asked, puzzled.
"I'm sure his maid is a good woman and I know all his children
are."[4]

A Simple Honorable Man, based on the life of the author's
father, tells about God's grace at work through an unself-
conscious saint.

In the rhythm of his week of worship and work the
Christian finds himself moving between his sources in
Christ and his services in the world. He finds himself freed
and opened in both directions. Sin is pierced so that he is
clear of that "vexed, beating, stuffed, and stopped-up brain,
heart or whate'er else." He is opened to resources and to
neighbor need. His consistency—poised integrity—is that of
the rubber tube made firm by a fluid's flow. At the same time

[4] *A Simple Honorable Man* (New York, Knopf, 1962), pp. 153–54.

he is clamped and bound at both ends. He is called by Christ and his neighbor, claimed by love through and through. He has become a channel of God's grace, but he knows only that he strangely finds gifts at hand which he can bestow upon the world about him. He bears the mark of his source; his style smacks of the style of Christ. Yet his inner consistency is but unshaped readiness and his pattern of habits is but disciplined and prepared openness for his tasks as Christ's ambassador and priest for the world.

Today no one can neatly sketch the lines of a Christian way of life for the decades that lie ahead. Yet even now certain clues expose themselves. Characteristically they take form as ministries of laymen to the world. They can be highlighted under four biblical images—suffering servant, light, salt, soldier.

SECTION THREE

His Ministry in the World

CHAPTER VII

SERVANT

"I wish that athwart the crossbar of every cross, on every altar of every church, there might be draped—a towel." Henry Hitt Crane makes this suggestion to point out that God revealed himself in Jesus Christ as a servant and that "the towel test" is the crucial evidence of Christian discipleship. In one of the most solemn moments of all history Jesus took the towel—symbol of service—and washed his disciples' feet, making it clear that this act epitomized his life and the lives of his followers (John 13:3–16).

The picture of the servant or slave is one of the controlling images of the New Testament to describe both Christ and the Christian community. Jesus, when he began his ministry and again later on, identified his task with the words of Isaiah describing the Messiah as one who preaches good news to the poor, release to the captives, sight to the blind, and liberty to the oppressed (Luke 4:18, Matt. 11:4–5). Repeatedly he asserted that he had come to serve and that his disciples were to follow his example in serving the needs of their neighbors (Mark 10:43–44, Luke 22:26–27). For the Christian to help a neighbor in need is to serve his Lord (Matt. 25:40). In the New Testament church they understood that loyalty to Jesus Christ bound them as slaves to all mankind. Christians are freed by the

Gospel in order to give themselves in concern to their fellow men (I Cor. 9:19). Luther caught this up into a tight paradox: A Christian man is the most free lord of all, and subject to none; a Christian man is the most dutiful servant of all, and subject to everyone.

What is more, the picture is clearly that of a suffering servant, one who sacrifices himself to bear the wounds of the world. Isaiah pictures the Messiah that way—ugly, bruised, despised, carrying our burdens and receiving our blows. Shortly after Jesus washed his followers' feet he moved on out to the cross to agonize and die for them and for us and for all mankind. This scene is central to the New Testament both as act and as symbol. Those who would follow Jesus are expected to take up a cross, to become a "living sacrifice," to express that best gift of God which is a love that suffers as it "bears all things" and "endures all things" (Mark 8:34, Rom. 12:1, I Cor. 13:7). As George Macdonald put it, "The Son of God suffered unto death, not that men might not suffer, but that their sufferings might be like His."

During the last war a British boy had to kill a young German soldier while carrying out his duties with a party of commandos raiding a French village. Since he was a Christian, he learned the German's identity and wrote to the mother thus deprived of her son. He asked for her forgiveness, stating that he hoped he could talk to her personally after the war. The German mother replied that she did forgive him since she, too, was a Christian. Then she invited him to visit her home in Germany "that you may take the place in my home, if only for a short time, of my son whom you killed." Compassion and forgiveness can shine through that tragedy which is seen in the light of the cross.

For the Christian all of life takes a cruciform pattern. In fact, if the mysterious Sphinx of the nearby Nile symbolizes the stubborn riddle of history and human experience, it is the cross of Calvary which presents the best answer. Justin, the famous second-century martyr, found the cross's features stamped upon every posture of man:

Think for a moment, and ask yourself if the business of the world could be carried on without the figure of the cross. The sea cannot be crossed unless this sign of victory—the mast—remains unharmed. Without it there is no plowing: neither diggers nor mechanics can do their work without tools of this shape. The human figure is distinguished from that of brute beasts solely by having an upright posture and the ability to exend the arms; and also by the nose through which the creature gets his breath, which is set at right angles to the brow, and displays just the shape of the cross.[1]

The Arc of Grace

The whole Christian ethic and the whole ministry of laymen are encompassed in just this—faith becoming active in love, faith translated into sacrificial living for others, faith thrusting to meet the pressing needs of men. "So this is now the mark," Luther asserted, "by which we shall certainly know whether the birth of the Lord Christ is effective in us: If we take upon ourselves the need of our neighbor." As Christ's life takes shape within us we become his imitators. Not his words and specific actions and special death but the whole pattern of his coming to earth sets our style of life as that of the servant-shape. The Christian life is the "faithful re-enactment of the servant-shape of God's act in Christ."

In the second chapter of Philippians Paul uncovers the mainspring and the inner workings of the Christian ministry when he says (verses 1–9, abbreviated): If there is any encouragement in Christ, any incentive of love, be of the

[1] *The Early Christian Fathers* (New York, Oxford, 1956), Henry Bettenson, ed. and trans., pp. 83–84, quoted in Roger Hazelton, *New Accents in Contemporary Theology* (New York, Harper, 1960), p. 135.

same mind. Have this mind among yourselves, which you have in Christ Jesus, who, though he was in the form of God, emptied himself, taking the form of a servant, being born in the likeness of men. And being found in human form he humbled himself and became obedient unto death, even death on a cross. Therefore God has highly exalted him.

Here we have the pattern, the style of Christ's life. It shows us God bending down to meet human need, the need of all humanity for salvation in the Son of God. We are to shape our lives according to the same pattern in respect to our neighbor's need. That is, we are to empty ourselves, identify with our neighbor and his need, live with that need, take the form of a servant in order to meet that need, suffer and in a sense die with that need, and rise again with that need through Christ. The arc of God's grace is followed and re-enacted by the arc of our deeds of love and service. We become a sort of Christ to our neighbor.

From this passage in Philippians the image of a servant can be divided into four phrases: (1) *Out of love for people* and (2) *at cost to oneself,* the layman ministers (3) by *identifying with human need* and (4) by *providing help.*

The Christian does not *consciously* serve people because Christ wants him to or because he serves Christ. That is, he is not *primarily* intent on doing his duty out of gratitude. Rather, he serves chiefly because he has become outgoing and has been caught up in a loving concern for those whom he meets. He has learned to love other human beings. Not always, nor perfectly. It is not that he likes everybody either. Yet he works steadily for the welfare of others, especially for those in obvious need and including the most unlovely ones. George Bernard Shaw once berated the English for considering the world a "moral gymnasium" in which to strengthen their own virtues, thus sometimes thinking about their "confounded principles" when they should be concerned with "other people's necessities."

Jim Morentz tells of talking with a bartender who in a confiding mood depicted how his childhood consisted of being shunted as an unwanted orphan from one institution to another. He finally met a woman who really showed love and concern for this lonely child. One day he asked the woman why she loved him. She replied, "Because God wants me to love you." For ten years after that, the bartender concluded, "I hated God." People want to be loved for themselves. The Christian loves not because of inner drives but because he is drawn to people and concerned about human needs.

Moreover, love is always costly. It always means involvement and expenditure. For a mother the care of her children may keep her from the careful grooming and smart appearance that were previously of great importance to her. Of course motherhood means fulfillment in the deeper sense. But self-fulfillment may not always be an obvious feature of a Christian's outgoing love. There is the famous story behind Albrecht Dürer's picture "Praying Hands." Sketched there are the gnarled hands of his friend. As struggling young painters these two had been so poor that one of them took up hard physical labor to support the other as he developed his artistic skill. By the time Dürer could support himself his friend had the hardened and unresponsive hands of a day laborer and had lost all chance to develop his talent as a painter. This theme—love as a living sacrifice—is a common one, yet each instance is a precious treasure. In the Christian tradition such sacrifice takes on additional meaning in its connection with Christ.

Dr. William N. Keith illustrated a Christian love both spontaneous and costly as he burned out his life for thirty-five years, serving mountainous Martin County, Kentucky, as medical doctor and general benefactor. Dr. Clair M.

Cook, in describing Dr. Keith's sacrificial life, calls him "A Schweitzer of the Mountains." His neighbors described him as "one hundred per cent Christian," one who could have been outstanding in his profession, except that for him medicine was "just a way of helping people."

Dr. Keith was willing to go anywhere in those mountains, often climbing on foot, and to tackle any medical situation with the crudest of improvised implements. He wiped out trachoma, virtually eliminated venereal disease, did countless tonsillectomies, vaccinations, and eye refractions. In one case he slept for thirty nights in the home of an infant with diphtheria to make sure a vital breathing tube would not be dislodged. Another time, in order to provide daily dressings for a badly burned child, he kept the child and its mother for weeks in a room fitted up in the barn with the needed facilities. To him his years of experience as a medical missionary now seemed like providential preparation for the rugged life and ready improvisations which his work in Martin County demanded. He never sent a bill but simply took what people could offer him.

The hearty nurse who joined him in his work, and then became his wife, soon found herself also caught up in all kinds of emergency medical acts. Just two months before Dr. Keith died in 1962 Martin County opened its new Health Center with nine full- or part-time staff members to continue the work begun by the Keiths as health officers. Stubborn as well as dedicated, Dr. Keith had from the start ignored public health department policies by mixing public health services with delivering babies and treating injuries and other acts that belonged to private practice. Though he was once fired by letter, his superiors finally had to let him go his own way, an exception to all rules who lived only by the Golden Rule. Many of his friends had to get used to the same single-mindedness, since, assuming that other people were as anxious to help as he was, he did not hesitate to commandeer any talent or possession which he thought someone should give to the current good work.

Dr. Keith's services to his people went far beyond the practice of medicine. For a tubercular patient he bought screens and built a porch. After one Christmas dinner he enlisted the men who were present to help put panes of glass into the broken windows of a needy home. He campaigned to secure the first fire truck for the town of Inez. He put together the first school bus for that area.

There was a flow of youngsters from the mountains to live at Dr. Keith's home, one by one, while they attended high school. He secured used schoolbooks from Pennsylvania, paying express charges himself. He also helped in the state-wide campaign for free textbooks by law. He arranged for a number of promising youngsters to get a college education. He used money he had inherited to aid in preparing medical missionaries. Struck by the ignorance concerning the Bible and the real spiritual darkness, he became an entirely volunteer Sunday-school missionary. He set up little schools in outlying areas and spent long Sundays making the rounds with any volunteer helpers he could press into service.

Identifying with Need

The Christian servant becomes completely involved in human problems. He tends to identify himself with the most extreme needs. When Jesus was asked "Who is my neighbor?" he responded with the story of the Good Samaritan. The answer: whoever stands in need is my neighbor. We are expected to empty ourselves of any advantage and to overcome any distance (in miles, in temperament, in cultural or ethnic separation) in this act of identification. The prophet Ezekiel once reported (3:15): "And I came to the exiles at Telabib, who dwelt by the river Chebar. And I sat there overwhelmed among them seven days." Father Damien reached his full ministry to those tortured unfortunates at the leper colony when he could one day begin to speak to them with the words "We lepers." So did the famous Latvian pastor, Traugott Hahn, after World War I when he chose to leave his family and enter the death house in order to be with his Communist-held parishioners and to face execution with them. Again, it is Christ who walks on ahead in this company. Countless Christians also join that company as they serve in less dramatic ways whereby some human being is grateful that another has been willing to "fellowship with my affliction" (Phil. 4:14, King James).

The Agony of God

I listen to the agony of God—
I who am fed,
Who never yet went hungry for a day.
I see the dead—
The children starved for lack of bread—
I see, and try to pray.

I listen to the agony of God—
I who am warm,
Who never yet have lacked a sheltering home.
In dull alarm
The dispossessed of hut and farm,
Aimless and "transient" roam.

I listen to the agony of God—
I who am strong,
With health, and love, and laughter in my soul.
I see a throng
Of stunted children reared in wrong,
And wish to make them whole.

I listen to the agony of God—
But know full well
That not until I share their bitter cry—
Earth's pain and hell—
Can God within my spirit dwell
To bring His kingdom nigh.

—GEORGIA HARKNESS[2]

Back in 1946 the *Saturday Evening Post* featured the remarkable story of Vera Emanuel. She was at one time an ordinary housewife and bridge-club matron who lived a well-to-do, happily married life in a small city in South Africa. But she was bored with her meaningless round of social activity, from bridge table to buffet luncheon to Friday Afternoon Uplift Society. After some soul-searching, and the reading of Paul de Kruif's *Microbe Hunters*, she decided to take up research in bacteriology. Soon she found herself swept into a six-year medical course, at the end of which she was a full-fledged doctor.

Now she chanced upon a black woman who had been one of her patients during her hospital residency. When the woman called her "Mis' lady Doctor," Vera Emanuel said, "I was seeing all the trusting black faces I had had under my care." Her mind was made up: she would start medical practice in Newclare, a Johannesburg slum which was one of the world's worst in terms of filth and danger, ugliness and hopelessness. Both people and living conditions were extremely primitive. Disease was rampant—tuberculosis and pellagra being particularly widespread among these blacks, half-whites, and Orientals. Here in these distressing circumstances Dr. Emanuel found a world of interesting personalities, a world that needed her sorely, a world she served with all that was in her. Though her work was bone-weary-

2 *World Communique*, May–June 1960.

ing amid dirt and physical danger, she stated that she would not think of exchanging it for the pallid pleasures of the bridge table. And all Newclare came to know and love her as Mis' lady Doctor or, better yet, Mother of Mercy.

It is blazingly clear that the full identification and involvement of the Christian with his neighbor both puts him at the mercy of that other human being and makes him vulnerable to the same evil or crippling onslaughts. To stand where the neighbor stands is to be in the same threatened condition. As Christians we stand weak and exposed in the world (Matt. 5:38–42). We are to be as sheep among wolves or lambs led to the slaughter (Matt. 10:16, Rom. 8:36). Dionysius of Alexandria, bishop of that city in the mid-third century, described the Christian reaction when plague ravaged that African city:

Most of our brethren did not spare themselves and held together in the closest love of their neighbors. They were not afraid to visit the sick, to look after them well, to take care of them for Christ's sake and to die joyfully with them. . . . Many of them lost their own lives after restoring others to health, thus taking their death upon themselves. . . . In this way some of the noblest of our brethren died—some presbyters, deacons and highly-esteemed lay people. . . . But the heathen did exactly the opposite. They cast out any people who began to be ill, deserted those dearest to them, threw the sick half-dead into the streets, and left the dead unburied.[3]

Boyd Payton, vice-president of the Textile Workers Union of America, Presbyterian elder, and highly respected resident of Charlotte, North Carolina, went to jail—together with seven union companions—several years ago, convicted of the charge of conspiracy to dynamite certain properties of the strike-bound Harriet-Henderson Cotton Mills in Henderson, North Carolina. Irregularities in the trial and the

[3] *Laity*, November 1957, p. 5, drawing on *The Ecclesiastical History of Eusebius*, vii, 22.

whole atmosphere of the incident have convinced many
people that Payton is telling the truth when he asserts his
innocence. In the *Christian Century* he was termed a
"Saintly Scapegoat." A widely circulated AP wirephoto,
taken when he appeared at the justice building for a lie
detector test during his imprisonment, shows him with man-
acles on his hands and the chain of a maxium-security strap,
though these devices are usually reserved for the most dangerous or psychotic prisoners. Payton himself has described
some of the indignities to which he and his companions
were subjected as they entered the prison.

However, Payton has also described how he suddenly lost
self-pity and realized that God was present with him in
prison. Immediately he saw that those around him needed
his help. And he found he could help these men because
he was in the same condition. First it was cigarettes and
talk. Later he conducted worship services right in his cell
block. At one of the chaplain's meetings there was a record
attendance when Boyd Payton spoke. He preached on love,
kindness, and understanding as the most powerful forces in
the world. Payton also started to teach inmates to read and
write. Sixty-nine men took part in his literacy classes, many
of them motivated to try to learn for the first time. He was
released from prison in 1961, and he says that those days
in jail were not only days of trial but also days when he
felt that God was close to him and gave him unusual opportunity to serve his fellow men.

Man's extremity is God's opportunity, so that it will be
through our very weakness as we take our place alongside
the needy that God's strength will be revealed. Our evident
frailty as earthen vessels makes us useful carriers of a
treasure that is thus clearly not our own (II Cor. 4:7). In
other words, it is through our emptying that we are able
to be helpful to a person in trouble. As we die with him,
Christ may raise us both from the dead. In less drastic

terms: as we put part of ourselves in exposed weakness into the situation, God may use our service to bring new hope or an answer.

Jim Elliot and his friends went unarmed into the jungles of Ecuador to convert the savage Auca Indians. Right away they met a martyr's death. But their act has thrillingly called forth support for his widow, Elisabeth Elliot, as she now succeeds in reaching these tribesmen with the message Jim had hoped to carry. The blood of the martyrs continues to be not only the seed of the church but also one way churchmen provide help for their fellow men.

Someone has likened our tight world to a dark cellar, part of which is flooded and the remainder packed with sixteen people. The one American has half of the world's "goodies." There is a gang of four or five toughs who want to seize these "goodies" and eliminate the American, while others support the American and have some good things of their own to preserve. All sixteen are armed with knives. Some have grenades which could destroy the cellar. Every man wants a grenade. When a missions executive related this parable to a friend, the quick retort was, "Yes, and you'd send a missionary into that cellar." "Well," the executive pointed out,

God did that. He sent His Son into the cellar. And they put Him to death; not just the gang, but all of them together. And out of the sacrifice of the Cross came the hope of the world.[4]

The Good Samaritan

The story of the Good Samaritan not only tells us who our neighbor is. It also provides the classic example of helpful, costly service. Here was a man who, despite his own travel plans, was open to a stranger, concerned about his

[4] John Coventry Smith, *Princeton Seminary Bulletin*, February 1961, pp. 40–41.

needs, and willing to sacrifice in order to identify with the needy one and to provide adequate help. Jesus contrasts this Samaritan sharply with two religious men who passed by so preoccupied or insecure that they refused involvement.

This is one biblical tale that can be transferred almost directly into modern city experience. A woman on a train is lost and separated from her appointed companion. She speaks a strange language and her foreign, helpless look has encouraged other passengers to sit at a distance from her. Her failure to produce a ticket stirs up an impatient conductor, whose shouts embarrass the whole carload of passengers. Most of them hide behind newspapers. One woman finally volunteers to speak the foreigner's language. She becomes enmeshed in the problem. Another traveler volunteers to pay the necessary fare, but then he retreats behind his paper. Several women apologetically explain that they cannot help because they have appointments to keep (perhaps at a church meeting).[5] The stage is certainly set for a good Samaritan with costly and patient ministrations.

Today there is frequent, sometimes desperate, need for emergency aid and a careful, time-consuming referral. True, welfare is complexly organized and the state takes vastly greater responsibility for "the soft areas of man's need." Yet immediate help in crisis and the personal touch of Christian concern are still much in demand.

For example, a clergyman of the Inner City Protestant Parish in Cleveland tells how a series of phone calls informed him that a woman had just given birth to her child in the emergency room of one of the fine private hospitals. As a welfare client she had to be transferred within a few hours to Metropolitan Hospital. But her family had no money to provide a taxicab and neither hospital had any fund for

[5] This story is adapted from a description in *Laity*, June 1956, p. 28.

such an emergency. There was a threat that she would be put out on the street. When the actual time of transfer arrived, a resident doctor at the private hospital personally paid for the cab. And the baby, who remained behind in an incubator, was improving, partly because a staff pediatrician had taken it upon himself to sit up all night next to the crib.

But welfare services by no means exhaust the layman's role in helping his neighbor. In fact, the churches have been much too willing to allow such a limited picture of the Christian's servant-task—as if it were fulfilled by charity to strangers. There are places—for example, on the streets of New Delhi or the Bowery—where one could not responsibly act like the Good Samaritan by answering immediate cries for help. Here he is called upon not only to give generously to support welfare agencies but also to spend himself sacrificially in relevant social action. As Walter Rauschenbusch put it:

The good Samaritan did not go after the robbers with a shotgun, but looked after the wounded and helpless man by the wayside. But if hundreds of good Samaritans travelling the same road should find thousands of bruised men groaning to them, they would not be such very good Samaritans if they did not organize a vigilance committee to stop the manufacturing of wounded men. If they did not, presumably the asses who had to lug the wounded to the tavern would have the wisdom to inquire into the causes of their extra work.[6]

The cup of cold water given in Christ's name is always a significant event. Its lengthened shadow falls upon the scene of the Last Judgment (Matt. 25:37-40). Countless acts of this quality contribute to the basic fabric of the layman's ministry. Nonetheless, Christians serve just as sacrificially in other ways as well. Luther once said that we Christians

[6] *Christianity and the Social Crisis* (New York, Association, 1917), p. 305.

must each day "creep into the cross of our vocation" within whatever circumstance we find ourselves. The servant image remains basic to the discussions of the next three chapters as these move beyond the Good Samaritan to develop other biblical images of Christian service or lay ministry.

CHAPTER VIII

LIGHT

"You are the light of the world," Christ tells his followers. But, then, Christ himself is *really* the Light of the world (John 1), and in the Nicene Creed we call him Light of Light. We are secondary lights. We are reflectors. Light is a gift we bear from God for the world. Centrally, the function of light is to reveal.

Under this image one thinks first of the Christian as an evangelist. It is his responsibility to tell people about Jesus Christ. One of the older evangelistic songs, by P. P. Bliss, came out of the author's experience in a storm-tossed ship seeking to make the harbor. The great lighthouse was a shining, welcome guide, but the many little harbor lights were missing, so the entrance was quite precarious. The song's refrain urges:

> Let the lower lights be burning!
> Send a gleam across the wave!
> Some poor fainting, struggling seaman
> You may rescue, you may save.

We are the lower lights, certainly.

No Obvious Beacon

Unfortunately, however, for most people in today's world Christ does not stand out as a great and obvious beacon. It is the ministry of Christians to let their reflected brightness point to Him Who is *the* light and yet is largely unknown (John 1:9–11). It seems fantastic that other men could look at us and see Christ, but that really is the Christian's calling. "Let your light so shine before men, that they may . . . give glory to your Father" (Matt. 5:16). We must point to Christ, show that in him something new and decisive has been added to the world, give evidence that that something has lighted us up. Like the electric bulb that is so immediately dependent on a source of power for its illumination. Like the candle in candlelighting ceremonies which so obviously sacrifices itself as it pours forth its borrowed rays. This is the layman's role as an evangelist, witnessing to his Savior, proclaiming Christ as his transfiguring Lord.

But such testimony is exceedingly difficult in the contemporary milieu. Just as modern men do not see any meaning in our corporate worship, so they do not hear words about another world, some third dimension, when they live a secular, two-dimensional existence. There must be a clear secular relevance for the Gospel. One World Council of Churches' study on evangelism declares that the "coming of Jesus Christ in the flesh and in the power of the Spirit is a 'secular' event. It is an event in the world and for the world. . . . It is the task of evangelists to rediscover and to proclaim the Gospel in its specific, concrete, unique and secular sense." Our talk of God and a Savior must apply quite directly to that flat world of modernity. It will be largely through deeds and a style of life that we can hope to provide such shafts of light.

Nor can our deeds point to ourselves and still be effective and enlightening signs. The glitter of our upright deeds will likely appear as deceptive tinsel to the cynics who deny all grace among men. Or the flashing brightness of the righteous ones will but dazzle and discourage and frighten the sensitive spirit who knows how shadowy is his existence. Besides, Christians seldom actually bring forth such nobility of character and action; their reflected light remains flickering and feeble.

Floodlighting the World

Since Christ is the light of the whole world, the layman's ministry is primarily to show how the world looks when flooded by that light. His task in the world is not centrally to point to his own bright personal experience, nor even to point to the light from which his experience came. It is rather *to point to the world as it is newly revealed in that light,* seen from this radiant perspective, enlightened by these fresh insights. The Christian moves into the world bearing a gift with which he can make more out of that gloomy and narrow place. It is as when the shade is raised in a previously darkened room or like the sun breaking through the clouds suddenly to brighten the whole setting.

He does not so much meet the nonbeliever by declaring a distant, exalted Savior, a mighty but invisible lighthouse or sun. Nor does he brashly set forth what Christ means in his own life. Rather, in his meeting with the other person, he, unconsciously perhaps, holds out promising possibilities for the tender psychic territory between them. He brings the light of Christ into the human relationship here being forged, weaving golden thread into the otherwise drab fabric of personal ties. He shifts from "what God has done for me" to "what God can do in our midst."[1] Similarly the

[1] Harry DeWire, *The Christian as Communicator,* p. 157.

light bearer carries new insights into every human relationship, every event, and every aspect of life. In other words he brings fresh perspectives to bear on the world.

After all, the main purpose of an electric bulb is to light a room, not to be looked at itself, nor to remind one of the powerhouse. And a little bulb or candle serves the whole room in which it is found. The New Testament pictures of the church always describe it as a small minority serving a larger whole. Today across the earth it becomes increasingly clear that that is the church's position—a tiny minority functioning for the whole world. In functioning as light bearer the Christian adds new vistas to the corridors of this time and of this place. With the eyes of faith and through a sanctified imagination he sees more in what is going on. He sees and reflects another dimension within today's human panorama. This too is evangelism.

Windows

Better than bulb or candle as the light image for laymen is the *window*. A window both points to the sun and reveals the room in that light. It is dependent on a source and is usually a minority feature of the room. Besides, it is self-effacing and provides perspectives from the outside. These last are the two focal features in the layman's ministry of light.

One looks through the best windows without seeing them. Christians cannot hope to be really transparent for Christ, but they can seek to be translucent, not entirely opaque and dull. The peculiar dimension of the Christian is precisely such translucency. The four characteristics of the Christian's dimension (see Chapter V) are all a readiness to show the world what it really is within its larger setting. The Christian is relatively free of self-serving in order to look at the world with frank and steady gaze. His poise enables him to view earthly pursuits with balanced and undistorted vision, knowing both their significance and their transiency. His own integration helps him to see the unity which underlies the whole world. His alertness allows him to discern God at work in every happening. And what he thus sees and knows enables the Christian as a suffering servant—or self-effacing window—to serve his Lord and his world as an opening through which God's revelation can penetrate God's world.

A major gift and task of the Christian layman, then, as of the window, is to minister by bringing ultimate perspectives to bear upon this world, to see it steadily "under the aspect of eternity." Only incidentally does the window point to the sun. Its central accomplishment is to light the room and provide a wider view. The proper window is the one that provides a sunlit room and an open glimpse of architectural balance in a unified total setting.

Modern Vistas

What helpful vistas does the Christian see when he looks at the world? This is too sweeping a question for the present discussion since it involves a theology of the world and could draw upon all the scriptural and historical insights of Christianity plus an analysis of contemporary culture. A few pointers and illustrations will have to suffice to indicate a general slant in response to this query.

From the Christian standpoint this world is not self-existent but belongs to One who made it, upholds it, and governs it. What is more, the Creator loves his creation; it is his first love and his fiancée, so to speak. In the Bible the first covenant God makes is with Noah and all living things. And God's last promise there concerns a new heaven and a new earth. Furthermore, all human life and invention, all nature and the elements, all space and the cosmos are declared to be one creation. At the hand of God they are fashioned into an integer, a universe.

Jesus Christ is at the heart of all these things; in him "all things hold together" and through him God would bring redemption to the whole cosmos (Col. 1:15–20). He is the light already shining from within. At the New Delhi Assembly of the World Council of Churches one committee declared:

Christ the Light did not remain outside the world to illumine it from above, but entered into human life, conquered the darkness and radiates light from within. This says to us that wherever we are in the world, God is there before us—the light is already there. The responsibility of the laity is to serve as reflecting mirrors or focussing lenses, to beam the light into all parts of the life of the world.[2]

Christians, then, will seek to reveal that this world is good, dependent, loved by its maker, a significant whole, and centered in Christ, its light.

These facts apply to the *modern* world, which sorely needs Christians who can light it up with such insights. Christians must be fully modern if they would serve as light bearers upon the contemporary scene. Too often church people have appeared to complain about each new trend, each changed feature, harking back in their ways of worship, their moral judgments, and their forms of speech to bygone eras. We live well within a radically transformed age, which has sometimes been called the "post-Christian era." Tragically, churchmen have not faced squarely into this new epoch.

Maurice Reckitt describes the church as an old-fashioned guest at a new-fashioned cocktail party: she is invited and treated politely, but everyone wonders why she dresses as

[2] *Laity,* February 1962, p. 29.

she does and why she comes at all when she understands so little of the bright conversation going on.

Today, in a technical age, dominated by the outlook of applied science, the Church seems often to have very little idea what the conversation *is* about. Its themes are not the sort of thing she was brought up to understand or even to be interested in. Hence either she tries to appear broad-minded and nods with uncomprehending politeness at what she supposes to be the brilliant things that are being said, or she adopts a superior air and tries to lift the conversation to what she assumes to be a higher plane . . .[3]

Relentless technological advance, fatalistic acceptance of machine rhythms for human lives, production systems that must constantly expand, men who are rootless hangers-on within vast organizations, obliteration bombs and interplanetary explorations, population explosions and urban wastelands—such technical and sociological factors present puzzling new experiences for our age. Technology is producing some machine answers. But these omnicompetent Frankensteins frighten us. Or we make them into gods. When we note the exploits of UNIVAC and EDSAC and ZETA, we wonder if these are the new gods who will go before us into the promised land.

Whereas the cathedral, visualizing that which is ultimately real, was the central symbol for a past society, our present society does not ask about reality so much as it demands a source of ready energy. Thus the atomic reactor is its fitting symbol. Jacob Bronowski, the scientist, has said, in effect,

For me the most significant building for our time is not the Cathedral but the Reactor. Here you can meet the scientist with his complete dedication to truth: here you can see the technician with his scrupulous attention to detail. Within a marvelously con-

[3] Maurice B. Reckitt, *Militant Here in Earth* (London, Longmans, Green, 1957), p. 51.

structed building you can discover a great company of devoted men bending their energies to a single purpose. Is not the Reactor the real symbol of our twentieth-century scientific culture?[4]

Of course, human sin has entered into modern technology just as readily as it has twisted and warped every other facet of God's world. Men worship the reactor's mystic blue flame and its power bursts without recognizing its Author. Or men use these awesome instruments of human invention to threaten and crush their fellow men rather than as servants of a common humanity. F. W. Dillistone has asserted that no part of the church's missionary task is more difficult "than the redeeming and sanctifying of this world of dynamos and reactors and computators and communications systems." Yet it is desperately important that the human spirit shall recognize God's presence in the midst of the most startling human explorations and gadgets.

A Social Passion

Joining technology as a second major feature of the modern age is the penchant for great social movements. Modern man has a *social passion*. If Christians would be light bearers they must show wherein this concern is a God-given gift. At his best the man of today is possessed of a burning desire for social justice; he puts fervor into his political commitments and gives an intense interest to current events, economic policies and international relations. Often he finds his personal destiny wrapped up in these matters. This means that he looks at life as a whole and is impatient with any word from the church that is partial in its meaning. It will not do to talk about a soul that is separate or about an individual who can enter the fuller life by pri-

---

[4] Quoted from a television program by F. W. Dillistone in Edward J. Jurji, ed., *The Ecumenical Era in Church and Society* (New York, Macmillan, 1959), p. 180.

vate decision. The modern man is seeking social salvation and organic integration within this world.

There are dangers in this fact, of course. One is the danger of exalting purely human achievements. Pandit Nehru, when he was opening the first link in a great new canal system, spoke of "viewing these projects where thousands of human beings are engaged in great constructive activity for benefit of millions of their fellow beings as temples and places of worship. These are sacred places—for me more sacred than temples, gurdwaras and mosques."[5] All too readily do men learn to worship their own efforts and their own grand schemes.

But the Christian errs when he says in effect: Since this is a collective age in which totalitarianism finds a place, since it is a day of vast social movements in which an evil Communism flourishes, therefore we must set our faces against this age and its trend toward social movements. Such a response evidences a lack of faith. God is at work in the twentieth century too. The Christian must find in the age, or bring to it, the divine intention behind this God-given social passion.

An English steel-plant manager became involved in a discussion group for managers sponsored by the Sheffield Industrial Mission (see the next chapter). His interest was caught by these monthly meetings in members' homes. Eventually he became the leader of a new group of the same type. Though he had been a Christian all his life, he is convinced that the industrial mission has opened up a new world of possibilities for him. "I look at things in a new light," he declares. He sees the moral and human dimensions of every managerial problem and is trying to discover what Christianity really means for his work. He believes that a manager should consider a wider range of factors in making

[5] Quoted by Dillistone in *ibid.*, p. 182.

decisions than most managers do by training and habit. He is also critical of those unrealistic executives who facilely speak of their company as one big happy family.

An Ohio physician attended a weekend conference for doctors which provoked some searching discussion of medical ethics and the doctor's responsibility in society. Afterward he admitted that he had in the past largely taken as authoritative whatever his medial associates within their professional organization had stated as policy. Now he was prepared to use a broader, more critical perspective and a more distinctly Christian outlook in his approach to the problems in his work world.

While some Christians stand at high places of decision and influence for interpreting modern technology and social isms, nearly all laymen have the same kind of responsibilities in their own localities and daily habitats. In the weekly round they will introduce or fail to introduce glimpses of an added dimension. Just as Paul once prayed that the earliest churchmen would be able to comprehend four dimensions (Eph. 3:18), so the Christian has the daily prayer that he may help all with whom he lives to glance occasionally into a new realm of possibilities. Let us illustrate this with brief reference to the Christian's role as citizen.

Political Insights

A famous German pastor of the last century, J. C. Blumhardt, when he studied with his men, alternated as his source material between the Bible and the newspaper in order to keep Bible reading related to concrete, contemporary events. Each Christian in his political life must try to bring these two sources together as he discusses headlines, as he votes, as he works for social justice and good government within his political party and in civic affairs. Not that he will try to read current events into the Bible.

Rather, he will try to apply biblical insights to passing happenings in order to extract their deeper meanings. This is the role of the prophet. Every Christian must bear that mantle in his own small or large world of political influence.

This does not imply that Christians as such have clear-cut answers to involved social issues when other men are in the dark. Political action in the arena of today's complex and technical society has about it an inevitable opaqueness. The rightness or wrongness of an act—and its very meaning— often remains but a cloudy conjecture. Many decisions can be made only by specialists or men who stand with power at the decision point. Blacks and whites shade off into grays, especially if one stands at a distance. But Christians grasp at least dimly the final meaning of it all. As friends of the master they know what he is doing better than the other workmen (John 15:15). They can focus shafts of light upon essential features of a complicated, befogged political scene.

Specifically, when the Christian enters into the power struggle (which he must do as a responsible citizen), he will bear with him into the fray at least these three flashes of insight. For one thing, men cannot finally mastermind political decisions and control history, since God is both at work within these processes and eventually rules over all social forces in the course of human events. Men are simply expected to exercise their best wisdom. Secondly, political parties and social systems are, under God, significant human undertakings, but they are all secondary. They are instruments to help in achieving human welfare and community. They also uphold human life so that men may live before their God. The Christian will resist all efforts to make any system absolute or total, because he can see that there is always something that lies beyond any human pattern.

Besides, in the third place, he can see that men constantly warp and selfishly misuse the best of causes and systems. Thus he will resist political (or any) fanaticism in himself and his associates. Though he works strenuously for the success of the cause and the party which he thinks best, he remains humble and will not attribute to himself or his friends any final wisdom or absolute rectitude.

In Leeds, England, a workman who was also shop steward for the union went into politics and became a city councilor. On the occasion of the baptism of one of his daughters several churchmen came into his home for a talk. As a consequence he became active in the church and felt that he had found an expression of Christianity which fitted right in with his ideas and actions as a socialist. He claims that he feels completely at home with the people of his parish, though many of them are political conservatives. Christianity has given him a greater understanding of things, so that he has come to see two sides to the political picture. "I suppose," he states, "this means that I am now more tolerant and flexible in my ideas."

Sometimes political groups do not welcome within their ranks those who can be tolerant and see another side to issues. A Christian may well suffer for providing such services to his group. But this is not a counsel of despair. As Robert McAfee Brown has pointed out, when we simply offer our best to God and trust that he will use it in ways which fit his own purposes

it relieves us of the intolerable burden of claiming that we have final wisdom, or can save the world with one more gimmick, or, more importantly, that what we are about to do politically is totally right and good. It releases us from these burdens and frustrations to work and strive and fight as significantly as we can, and not to be too importantly self-righteous about it.[6]

These truths apply with equal force to the layman's ministry at home, at daily work, and in his leisure activity. He

[6] Robert McAfee Brown, *Christianity and Society*, Winter 1955, p. 26. The political insights described above are also found in this article.

brings the same understanding of the world right into the
room where he works or plays, providing windows over
the workbench, the kitchen sink, and the bowling lanes. He
will minister to that segment of life—those people and things
—where he stands daily.

It will be secular life; these will be temporary relationships and transient things—processing food, selling insurance, washing dishes, bowling. The layman ministers by
relating secular things to God. He represents these matters
as the bearers of God's creation and therefore good. His
actions try to show that Christ's death has somehow made
these things look different. He knows and reveals that
Christ's Second Coming strangely casts upon the scene a
lurid light that both heralds a rosy dawn and trumpets the
fires of destruction.

A professor of journalism in Chicago has recently
awakened to the fact that the large university in which he
teaches is his parish. He had not previously sensed the relationship between his daily work and his discipleship. Now
he finds he can really communicate on a deeper level with
people, not only in his formal classroom teaching, but in
all his relationships. He sees his work and his contacts as
part of a ministry. He says that for the first time he is talking to fellow faculty people about the basic values of life.
Since his profession has become a mission he sees so much
more in it and so much more to do through it.

Against the dense, stuffy seriousness of those who would
make transient things ultimate, the Christian can open up,
lighten, relativize. He can add humor; he can show that these
things are not final, that there is something beyond. On the
other hand, against those who cynically devaluate earthly
pursuits, the Christian can make these things transparent to
God's presence in them so that they are transfigured and
shown in their true value as veils of God. Thus, the paper
money of our modern world can be recognized as the coinage

of the eternal, as George MacLeod puts it. God is at work in his whole world if laymen but have the eyes to see him and if they can only be windows to reveal his presence there.

The World of Nature

But the need of the hour, according to some of the most penetrating thinking of our day, is a fresh awareness of the close connection between Christ and the natural world. When the World Council of Churches met at New Delhi in 1961, one speech on the central theme—Christ the Light of the World—insisted that under this banner churchmen must realize "that Christ cannot be a light that lighteth every man coming into the world, if he is not also the light that falls upon the world into which every man comes." The speaker, Joseph Sittler, was proclaiming that one understands redemption in Christ only when that doctrine "swings within the larger orbit of a doctrine of creation."

This emphasis upon God's natural creation is especially needed in the twentieth century. Not only has a secular age tried to push God out of his world, but also a technical and urban age has cut man off from nature. Today men know nature only as the stuff for human use or abuse. It is real estate to be cleared for new suburbs or it is raw material to be split open for a fantastic energy that will run man's machines or obliterate his enemies. Sittler speaks of atoms "disposable to the ultimate hurt," referring to "nature's pathetic openness to glorious use or to brutal rapacity." He holds up some lines of Gerard Manley Hopkins, nineteenth-century poet, that celebrate "the world as a God-haunted house":

> The world is charged with the grandeur of God.
> It will flame out, like shining from shook foil;
> It gathers to a greatness, like the ooze of oil

Crushed. Why do men then now not reck his rod?
Generations have trod, have trod, have trod:
   And all is seared with trade; bleared, smeared with toil;
   And wears man's smudge and shares man's smell: the soil
Is bare now, nor can foot feel, being shod.

"This radioactive earth," Sittler concludes, "so fecund and so fragile, is [God's] creation, our sister, and the material place where we meet the brother in Christ's light. Ever since Hiroshima the very term *light* has ghastly meanings. But ever since creation it has had meanings glorious; and ever since Bethlehem meanings concrete and beckoning."[7]

The layman's ministry in the world includes recognition that nature is God's handiwork, a part of Christ's realm of redemption, and therefore "our sister." Through our attitudes toward physical elements, the soil, and growing things, through many little or large acts we reflect to our neighbor a judgment about the nonhuman world.

The Christian's role in the twentieth century compares to that of St. Francis in the thirteenth century, though in less spectacular ways. Francis, fool for Christ, could welcome searing fire as his brother and the fair moon as his sister and the birds as congregation for his preaching because he lived intimately with their common Father and their Elder Brother. This was a new departure after centuries of the Dark Ages, when the forces of nature were feared as harsh tyrants or worshiped as mysterious, untrustworthy gods but were seldom known as fellow creatures of God's good earth. G. K. Chesterton sees Francis' fresh appreciation of nature as the dawn of a new day:

While it was yet twilight a figure appeared silently and suddenly on a little hill above the city, dark against the fading darkness. For it was the end of a long and stern night, a night of

[7] Joseph A. Sittler, "Called to Unity," *The Ecumenical Review*, January 1962, pp. 178–87.

vigil, not unvisited by stars. He stood with his hands lifted, as in so many statues and pictures, and about him was a burst of birds singing; and behind him was the break of day.[8]

The call in our time is for Christians who can light the pathway of modern man into appreciation of all nature and the cosmos as veils of the glory of the Lord Jesus Christ.

The Measure of Man

However, any scrutiny of the link between Christ and this world misses its own key concept if it does not highlight the *Incarnation,* wherein God took on complete *human* nature, giving brilliance and fulfillment to that central facet of creation which is man. In Jesus Christ, the God-Man, divinity suffused humanity with new light as glowing fire permeates iron in the red-hot ingot at the steel mill. In the incarnation God's fires tempered and refined human nature. In that act our nature became malleable so that it could accept the blows of suffering and crucifixion and come forth a new, resurrected being, forged into the perfect link between heaven and earth, between God and a sinful race of mortal men.

That link, with its curve of grace, takes shape in the Christian who bears "the New Being" after the pattern of Christ's incarnation, crucifixion, and resurrection. What does this mean for the layman's role as light bearer?

It means that Christ is the measure of humanity, that what is revealed through scripture to believers has a helpful relevance for the whole human panorama. It is up to Christians to dig out that meaning as they dig into the world's needs. Across the portal of one of the creative centers for modern evangelism, the Evangelical Academy at Loccum in Germany, are chiseled these words from Colossians: "In Christ

[8] G. K. Chesterton, *St. Francis of Assisi* (Garden City, Doubleday, 1957), pp. 36–37.

are hid all the treasures of wisdom and knowledge" (2:3). If they are hidden, they will not shine forth like glaring headlines; these treasures must be searched out.

By way of illustration let us turn to three instances in the modern world of laymen witnessing to our common humanity. The first one hints at what the inspiration of Jesus Christ can contribute to the contemporary necessity for men to live together in harmony. The second points toward a Christian service to contemporary culture. The third shows what one can see in the lives of earth's poor when he knows that Christ is in their midst.

In the various provinces of the Netherlands the Reformed Church has developed resourceful conference centers devoted to teaching people how properly to live with one another. Each center is called a *Vormingcentrum*, which means a place for the growth of the total personality.

Typically, a mixed group of about thirty people—many of them not churchmen—will meet for a week in a large, rambling house to learn to live together. In the name of Christ these centers nurture *Mitmenschlichkeit*, brotherliness. For example, one group at "De Haaf" will spend a week studying France. As the participants research informally and discuss French foods, cathedrals, art, and cities, they come to know each other and learn to get along together. Then the following week they set out to tour France by bus—a real test of brotherliness—and learn also to appreciate the people and life of this neighboring nation. Or a group of teacher candidates will learn to express themselves more clearly by practicing sociodrama, pantomime, and story mime.

The setting for whatever goes on is the Christian community. The emphasis is on helping people treat others as human beings without trying to use or ignore one another. The participants have a chance to begin sharing life experiences, to open up, be receptive, trust other people. They may begin to sense what genuine human community is all about. Significantly, these centers have no special chapel buildings. Informal worship is held in the *living* room!

At one of these Dutch centers, an old castle near Leyden called Oud Poelgeest, Director A. W. Kist conducts conferences that provide some arresting human experiences. Kist believes that after generations of hatred, deep distrust, and mutual destruction in the European countries, culminating in the holocaust of World War II, Europe should be integrated into a new community. But this, he insists, will depend on a new European's coming into being, one who is opened and brotherly. However, such a happening can be based only upon the New Being in Christ and a new coming together in which men can drop their defenses and remain open to each other.

Director Kist finds a parable of Europe's evolution in the history of his own castle. Once it was a fortress surrounded by a moat, providing defense for one family against all comers. Then it became a private home with a carriage house and broad gardens, the homeland from which one family sallied forth into the social life of Leyden. For a while it was deserted, and then in recent decades it was occupied by foreign troops, quite paralleling the soul of Europe in this twentieth century. Now it has become the meeting place and community center for as many as six thousand people in a year. Its dormitory, the House of Metamorphosis, carries upon each room the name of some great city—Rome, Athens, Thebes—whose culture helped to build European civilization. These grounds now serve in the mental and emotional preparation for a new phase, European integration. Here men learn social wisdom, how to meet as persons and grow into meaningful community.

Conferences at Oud Poelgeest build social wisdom out of many ordinary experiences. A new awareness of God's world and human need arises from the experience of uncertain expectancy which comes to strangers as they try to settle in with one another in a queer old castle, finding where and with whom they will eat and sleep and associate for a week. Some are bold and careless as they leave their valuables in the common dormitory; others timidly hide their watch and money. At a large dinner table each is constantly passing small serving dishes to others, learning interdependence in the providing of our daily wants. Participants create a community of co-operation as they peel potatoes, sweep floors, and do the other household chores, each person doing a job on behalf of his new companions. They spend time together working on drama, art, and speech; listening together; and sharing a fellowship of silence. In all these experiences they are finding Christian meaning and Christian methods for learning to live together.

Occasionally a group of coal miners comes to the castle, men filled with suspicion toward strange people and much talk. Director Kist, in a chalk talk, pictures the house of human relations and shows how men choose to hide in private cells in the cellar when there are many fine living rooms which could be enjoyed together if we would try trusting each other. In a few days he has the miners moving out of their cell attitudes, ready to unfold new reaches of their common humaneness.

Carrying Jesus Christ into the life of human community is not, of course, confined to such conference centers. Just as in the early Middle Ages the church became by necessity the civilizing and humanizing influence among the barbarians of western Europe, so at many places in modern society Christians have the opportunity to serve a similar purpose. In many an "asphalt jungle" within huge modern cities Christians who are ready light can point the way toward community stability through an informal "house-church" or through organized activity within a given block of slums. This is happening, though far too infrequently.

Christ within Culture

In Sweden a student Christian movement during the first decades of the twentieth century swept on to the craggy hills of the ancient town of Sigtuna several clusters of attractive Greek-style and monastery-like buildings. Facing Lake Mälar and accompanied by massive stone ruins of churches which mark the first Christian inroads upon Sweden in the eleventh century, the Sigtuna Foundation is devoted to the service of contemporary culture in Christ's name. Situated several score miles from Stockholm and from Uppsala, it is both accessible and sufficiently secluded to function as both a place of retreat and a crossroads of intellectual currents.

The Sigtuna Foundation has a forty-year history of service to the broad reaches of Swedish national life. In a day when the Church of Sweden (Lutheran) was bound fast to the nineteenth century through petrified traditions and a trussed-up interpretation of Scripture, the original student movement made the exciting discovery that God was at work in present events. The students claimed that the Gospel "surges like a tidal wave" through some of the modern trends which were bypassing an introverted church. They challenged all Sweden to intellectual combat. Under the leadership of Manfred Björkquist they also made a sustained approach to the disaffected workingmen.

From the start it was felt that the center at Sigtuna should be a meeting place for every kind of idea and group and aspiration. Economics and politics and culture, as well as religion—indeed any subject of importance to the Swedish people—were included in its concerns and formed the basis for conferences in which all viewpoints could be heard within the free setting of a Christian home. There are no closed gates at the Sigtuna Foundation. In another metaphor: it is an instrument with a wide register. While the movement and its home have clearly been an expression of the church's life, they have never been subject to direct ecclesiastical control. Thus they have remained free for radical experimentation in the name of Christian service to human culture.

At the beginning a People's College or folk high school was established. Inspiration for this school comes from the Grundtvigian adult-education movement, motivated by the Christian humanism caught in the dictum of that nineteenth-century Danish Bishop, N. F. S. Grundtvig: "First man, then Christian." The school brings to Sigtuna annually more than a hundred young people who have been earning a living and now wish several months of study aimed at fostering more independent thinking and a better grasp of the issues of modern life.

A gracious guesthouse provides the quiet beauty, relaxed schedule, and Christian home atmosphere which attract many secular people for a few days or a few weeks of rest or concentration. No small proportion of modern Swedish literature is composed at this place, since poets and other creative artists find it a favorite haunt. An extensive library provides resources for researchers who seek opportunity for quiet, concentrated work.

On a neighboring pine-clad hill are planted "a couple of temples from the Acropolis," which form the Humanistic School. Here are blended Christian and classical humanism into an education for boys and girls under principles akin to those of the church academies in an earlier America.

Various conferences provide one of Sigtuna's most significant Christian contributions to Swedish national life. As early as the 1920s, when Swedish industrial life was marked by conflict, Sigtuna brought workers and employers together to talk over difficulties in a favorable atmosphere. Over the decades there have been many gatherings for workers, for students, for poets, for doctors, for architects. Sometimes theologians participate, sometimes they do not; but professional churchmen never dominate these "contact" conferences. The Gospel receives a hearing, but discussion is always open. Conversion is not the aim; meeting the voiced needs of people in society is the central concern.

In the early 1950s, when the Kinsey reports on the sex habits of Americans provoked an ill-informed, unhealthy public controversy in Sweden, Director Olov Hartman called together leading doctors, sociologists, and churchmen for discussion which succeeded in clearing the air and raising the level of debate on the issues involved.

Today the Christian humanism at Sigtuna remains open to new cultural trends and new opportunities to serve. Hartman believes that the church should open the sluices for the needs of the world and the glory of life. Let the Gospel burn unsheltered, he urges, with open flames amid the currents of our time. Sigtuna works more with cultural leaders and the arts, rather than pursuing its earlier function among industrial people and social problems. One present-day emphasis is religious drama, with Director Hartman a major author of liturgical plays. Each summer young people gather at Sigtuna from the national network of drama circles that is called the Foundation for Liturgy and Drama. Rigorous workshops train these people in a kind of religious drama that has its effect upon the contemporary trends in the secular Swedish theater. Annually in August there will be repeated outdoor productions of a play.

One year, for example, Hartman's *The Fiery Furnace* was presented. It was full of visual and verbal symbols. There was much choral speech. The audience was considered to be a congregation and to be involved in the action, which took place before an altar and before God. Based upon Daniel and Revelation, it was the story of the conflict between Christianity and a hostile, totalitarian state. Three men were put through a "fiery trial." The right side of the altar was the realm of the church and the left that of the state. One man threw off the black robes of the state and repudiated it. He was cast into prison. Now his wife accused him of neglecting his family, since, lacking the mark of the beast (i.e., the sign of religious obedience to the state), she could no longer buy bread. Another man stepped from the church to put on the black robe of the state. At the end, playwright Hartman came to the altar garbed in his ecclesiastical robes as a priest of the state church of Sweden. There followed a brief worship service. Since worship anticipates the end of the world and Christ's complete triumph, those actors wearing the black robes of the state took them off as a sign of conversion. All of this was accomplished with an imagination and artistic skill which commend the play to the best circles of Swedish drama.

Christ is the measure of mankind. Director Olov Hartman caught something of this truth when he said, while describing the Chapel at the Foundation, "If the cultural work of the Foundation is such that nothing human remains strange to its endeavors, if nothing is considered too profane or too blasphemous to have the right to express an opinion in the discussions and conferences, this is because the Chapel leads us into the gospel where everything human is suffered and reconciled."[9] Sigtuna's activities are saying this with many voices.

Christ among the Poor

The third illustration of what it means to call Christ the measure of humanity is found in the experience of a young graduate of Harvard Law School who has spent more than six years immersed in the "squalor, depression, poverty and

[9] Olov Hartman, *The Sigtuna Foundation* (London, SCM, 1955), pp. 36–37.

frustration" that is east Harlem. He lives as his neighbors do amid "smells of sweat and waste, bathtubs in the kitchens, direct current, predatory vermin, secondhand clothes, a million empty beer cans in the gutters." His legal counsel in that place is "as much a vehicle of pastoral care as it is the practice of law." Not only has William Stringfellow carried out a layman's ministry, for Christ's sake serving and enlightening those he can reach. He has also learned of Christ's hidden presence among the poor. He points to several evidences which are discernible to the eyes of faith.

For one thing, since "men live at each other's expense," the aggravated sufferings of the poor provide a service "to all those who suffer less and to all those who are not poor." For example, they become expendable labor upon which the rest of us build. The poor represent the rest of us in this manner. More significantly, the suffering of the poor clearly "bespeaks the power and presence of death among men in this world." Their constant proximity to death portrays the true condition of all men.

From this proximity to death blossoms "a radical and wonderful piety," a "most remarkable social morality." The members of a slum gang are willing "actually to risk their lives for each other, and for their society, and for causes which outsiders would think unworthy—like jurisdiction over a street that is filled with garbage or over a girl who probably is not a virgin." These kids "have the freedom to offer their lives for another in spite of the undeservingness of the one for whom the offer is made. That is strangely reminiscent of the gospel, in which One offers his life for all, even though none are worthy of his life."

Furthermore, Stringfellow believes, Christ is hidden in the most hopeless human case. He describes a drug addict whom he has befriended. The boy "stops in often on Saturday mornings and shaves and washes up, after having spent most of the week on the streets." His father threw him out;

he has repeatedly run afoul of the law; he has worn out his welcome with social workers by making suckers of them. His health is broken; he is entirely unlovable. "He is dirty, ignorant, arrogant, dishonest, unemployable, broken, unreliable, ugly, rejected, alone. And he knows it. He knows at last that he has nothing to commend himself to another human being. He has nothing to offer." But here is embodied the situation of us all, for before God we are all unlovable and without anything to offer. "Hidden in the obnoxious existence of this boy is the scandalous secret of the Word of God," for God has loved us under just such circumstances, and he loves this boy as well.

What is missing, except in the presence of a few people like William Stringfellow, is the concerned community of those who know and proclaim the yet-hidden Gospel. What is called for, Stringfellow declares, is that Christians shall come among the poor in their own poverty with nothing to offer "except the power to discern and the courage to expose the gospel as it is already mediated in the life of the poor."[10]

William Stringfellow is unusual and his ministry is quite dramatic, even radical. But the same kind of awareness and sensitivity to the human element in depressed people can take shape among ordinary people in less conspicuous ways. In Chicago at Cabrini Homes, a housing development which has had real success in racial integration, a white janitor named York was watching his children play at a playground when he saw a group of teen-age Negro boys slug a white boy. He caught the boys and called the police. But he did not let it go with that. Instead he followed those boys with his help through their court experiences. One boy had a bad record and it took months to straighten out his case, yet York stuck with it. When asked why he bothered, he

[10] *The Christian Century*, May 10, 1961, pp. 584–86.

simply said, "I'm interested in kids; I got two of my own."

On Riker's Island stands a New York City correctional institution for men and boys. Outside the fences of the penitentiary are two cottages, which provide a "Cottage Program." Mr. Robert Nadel, dedicated young housefather, takes some pride in showing visitors his cottage and its program. Those boys with a record of good behavior in the institution come to live for twelve weeks in these cottages—about thirty-six at one time—without bars, locks, or uniformed guards, in a community atmosphere which requires some group responsibility. The cleanness and neatness, the schedule and semiprivacy are new to many of these products of the city slums. It is up to housefather Nadel to inspire in these boys some sense of integrity and self-respect. He is devoted to the effort to cultivate the best humanity within each boy that comes into his cottage. This is discouraging work. Mr. Nadel believes—as do many penal authorities—that there should be a larger number of halfway houses, removed from the prison, for those who have just been released from the penitentiary. Halfway houses provide some of the same helpful atmosphere as do the Riker's Island cottages, but in the more likely context of the freedom and responsibility of a citizen in society.

A medical doctor in Indiana has a number of Negroes among his patients. One Negro father could not pay his bill, so the doctor asked him to do some carpentry work. In working together, these two became more deeply identified with each other. The doctor gained insights into his friend's needs and the needs of that man's home. Over a year's time he has been teaching that family personal hygiene and even how to cook. The doctor helps the other man handle his pay check in order to pay bills and to provide proper foods for balanced meals.

Of course, William Stringfellow and these other persons cited not only illustrate how a Christian can gain deeper insights and help to light up our common humanity. They also illustrate how Christians can help others. They not only point to the presence of the Christ who is there. They also *bring* Christ and the Gospel as they befriend other people, identify themselves with the most needy, and try to help. It is a matter not only of seeing but also of identifying and doing. It is not only a process of revelation but also a process of permeation and redemptive change. Here the analogy of salt is more apt than that of light.

CHAPTER IX

SALT

Dispersion

"You are the salt of the earth," Christ tells his disciples. Obviously the Christian's saltness comes from Christ. But salt serves its purpose as it loses itself in the soup or permeates the meat. Here is the emphasis upon dispersion. Laymen must scatter themselves and enter thoroughly into all parts of the world to which they minister. They will want to identify themselves with the world's causes and preoccupations, expending themselves as they enter into the struggles and serve the needs of their many neighbors, immersed in all kinds of secular stew—politics and civic affairs and business enterprises and mass entertainment and vacation projects and youth activities and the rest of it. Ultimately our home is in heaven, but our role on this earth carries us into eager participation in this world and close association with secular-minded people. When salt is put on meat it disappears—or else it isn't working! Better than light, this figure of salt represents the quality of penetration and identification with the world.

It is exceedingly difficult for most middle-class, suburban or farm Protestants to reach out toward people whose world mien is foreign to their own, those in serious difficulty or those who look and act differently—especially the very rich or the very poor, manual laborers, migrant workers, criminals, the mentally ill, offbeat intellectuals, and the intelligentsia. The worlds of these people are very distant in language and thought from the world of the typical churchman.

When Horst Symanowski became pastor of a parish at Mainz-Kastel in Germany, he was determined to know the daily life of his parishioners. He took a job in the cement factory where most of them worked, without telling his immediate fellow workers who he was. One day one of these men discovered he was a preacher and registered surprise. Symanowski invited him to attend church, and he agreed that he would like to see what his friend did on Sunday. With great care the pastor prepared his sermon to reach that one man, choosing subject and language to fit his particular situation. The factory worker was present and heard the sermon. But when Symanowski met him later in the week and asked for his reaction the man shook his head and confessed that he had not understood one word of it. Then Symanowski started to realize what a restrictive ghetto is church life and how great is the distance to the life of much of mankind.

Symanowski persisted and became famous for his successful ministry to factory people. One of his techniques was discussion of his sermon with a group of day laborers before he undertook to preach it. His experience underscores the need of the church to reach out consciously and strenuously into many segments of the modern world. Salt does not serve its purpose in the box on the shelf. Today salty Christians need to be shaken out with vigor!

Remembering Paul's admonition that Christians are to be "all things to all men" (I Cor. 9:22), American Protestants have in a number of instances begun to move out with a Christian ministry to people and places quite "distant" from the church. Usually they take on the forms of life and protective colorations of the groups with which they identify.

Well-known instances include a San Francisco ministry to beatniks by Pierre Delattre, Jazz Pastor John Gensel in Greenwich Village, Malcolm Boyd's "espresso nights" for Colorado intellectuals, and the Church of the Saviour's coffeehouse in downtown Washington.

There are many other examples, most of them quite unheralded. Some clergymen are seeking factory experience. Two graduates of Princeton Seminary worked for several years on the assembly line at the Cadillac plant in Detroit. Some Christian colleges are beginning to rediscover that they have a distinctive mission within that difficult academic world in which they are struggling and seeking to achieve and to serve. Sometimes the campus Christian ministry at a university takes on a daring outthrust—for example, the Christian Faith and Life Community in Austin, Texas.

Evangelical Academies

The lay training centers of postwar western Europe, perhaps seventy in number, have been outstanding experiments in permeating the world. They are the church patiently listening to the world; they blend evangelism and social action in a fresh and vigorous reaching out on the part of the church into many areas of the secular, common life.

In Germany, for example, some eighteen conference centers, called Evangelical Academies, have emerged since the nightmares of Hitler's Third Reich. Recent years have brought to these academies as many as forty thousand participants attending some seven hundred conferences annually. In their first fifteen years the academies helped to change German public life significantly, to provide a fresh hearing for Christian ideas in factory, market place and forum.

Basically the academies are conference centers that serve

the public interest in the name of the church. A typical
three-day meeting will provide a few first-class lectures and
considerable frank, open discussion of the issues that confront men in daily work or in social and political life. Many
of the leaders in German society participate, some of them
contributing a thoroughly secular viewpoint. All shades of
opinion find free expression. Here churchmen make contact
with secular segments of society and learn to listen to the
experiences and problems of modern men. Here the church
performs a public service by providing a neutral platform
for honest encounter of mind with mind and person with
person across all the emotional and technical barriers in a
complex social structure. Within the free atmosphere of a
Christian home churchmen participate in creative dialogue
with the world primarily through the method of open discussion. Essentially these academies are bridgebuilders, tying
together the church and the world, forging links between
various segments of an unintegrated civilization, providing
outreach and relevance for the Christian faith in all segments of human existence.

Many of the conferences are for particular occupational
groups. There have been gatherings for such groups as the
following: mayors, journalists, soldiers, refugees, doctors,
midwives, nurses, teachers, students, industrial workers, social workers, salesmen, and apprentices. Problem-centered
conferences have dealt with a wide variety of the issues and
interests of modern men—Russia today, modern jazz, contemporary clothing fashions, East-West tensions, the future
of the village, the prosperity of West Germany, the responsibilities of dancing teachers and night-club enter-
tainers, etc. When academy representatives approached
dancing teachers they discovered that these people were
aware of carrying considerable responsibility for the education of teen-agers and were quite open and eager for the

help which academy programs and people could give for their occupation.

Occasionally academies reach out with their services into the neighboring cities. At times the Evangelical Academy at Bad Boll in Württemberg has featured campaigns aimed at building up community life and morale in a given city. Into that locality it sends a corps of specialists much like a Billy Graham team. But instead of holding huge evangelistic rallies, the corps conducts as many as forty conferences in two weeks, hoping to involve each person in the community three times—as a family man, as a citizen, as a worker. There are technical discussions in the fields of sanitation, hospitals, industries, political machinery, artistic and cultural pursuits, family life, and the like. Christian commitment, zeal, and understanding are brought to focus on these secular matters.

The academies are usually concerned to follow through with their participants. Several of the larger ones have nearly a hundred "house circles," groups with academy experience who meet regularly in their home city for fellowship and discussion, sometimes for Bible study and social-action projects. Some of these circles are occupational groups or cells within a given factory or industry.

These academies, paralleled by similar developments in Europe and America and elsewhere, are a significant illustration of the way Christian influence can move out into every part of the human enterprise in our modern world.

The Bad Boll Academy has specialized in conferences for factory people from the nearby industrial cities of Württemberg. One camera firm had refused to co-operate in sending its people to such conferences, though a scattering of them had attended on their own initiative. Finally a staff member from Bad Boll got a young left-wing socialist, who as head of the board of shop stewards was a full-time union representative, to attend a conference for shop stewards. He became so enthusiastic that he enlisted management and employees alike to attend a conference for that factory, called a Cross-Section Conference because it included representatives from all echelons within a particular factory. That camera firm, as a consequence, has become quite co-operative with Bad Boll programs. The young socialist, though he stays away from the organized church, serves the church in the factory, lectures often at Bad Boll, and has become virtually a volunteer staffman for that academy.

An administrator in the city government of Stuttgart watched Bad Boll's work with industry and decided there should be similar conferences for government people. He gathered thirty of his friends and asked one of the Bad Boll staff to explain their work. This man led in bringing department after department of the Stuttgart government into Bad Boll conferences. A year later this work had grown to the point that Bad Boll called a full-time man onto its staff for work with public administrators.

At Sheffield in England after World War II Canon (now Bishop) E. R. Wickham began an Industrial Mission which has come to involve a staff of more than half a dozen specially trained clergymen. These men cultivate an imaginative and loving service to steel-plant life. After clearing with management and union authorities, they began to visit the great steelworks of Sheffield, patiently and persistently visiting people on all levels of factory life. They visit in offices, in shops, and in homes. They have formed friendships with many men who have been entirely outside the orbit of the church's influence. They approach these people through a context entirely different from the appeal of the usual parish or congregation. Yet the clergymen move beyond knowledge of these people in the steel-plant functions and come to know them as individual human beings and as friends. After good will and trust are developed it becomes easier to initiate projects and workers start to assume that such a mission is natural for the church.

At Sheffield it became possible to visit men regularly, both as individuals and as groups, in melting shops, mills, foundries, forges, machine shops, and offices. The clergymen were able at some places to visit men during work periods, more often during lunch break and shift changes, or after work hours. The gatherings are quite informal, both humorous and serious, very broad in the subjects discussed. Out of them emerge projects and informal groups in which Christians and non-Christians combine to broaden worker prospectives through courses and discussion, to improve working conditions, or to provide greater good will and co-operation in the joint enterprise of producing steel. Though these contacts have a personal meaning that goes deeper than simply education, the Mission does make a significant contribution to the training and educational programs within the steel industry. Many leaders in that industry, conceiving of their corporations as great, complex communities of people engaged in a common project, are aware of the need to face together the difficult social, political, and even philosophical questions that their tasks raise. Many of them welcome any help theology can give. Most of the large steelworks in Sheffield regularly send men to residential training conferences that focus upon theology, are organized by the Mission, and are the only training projects that include both management and work people.

The best fruitage of the Industrial Mission is the development of lay leadership within the plants and the emergence of "lay projects" initiated and carried almost entirely by the steel-plant people. A senior manager may convene fellow managers to study their common problems. A young manager may invite a dozen other young managers into his home from time to time. Or an apprentice will organize a meeting with a speaker for other apprentices. These groups remain open to all comers and are not composed primarily of Christians, yet the Christian perspective will find a hearing on a given problem. This is the goal toward which the missioners work, considering themselves as fuses laid to the barrels of gunpowder. Incidentally, the same kind of industrial mission is developing in Detroit and elsewhere in the United States.

Most of the laymen who are discovered as leaders do not want to identify themselves with a parish. Take, as an example, a worker in the progress department of a large steel mill in Sheffield. Though he "hadn't much time for the church," he was attracted by the approach made by the industrial missioners and admits that his life has been strongly influenced by the mission. He thinks of himself as a "little rabbit" in earlier days; now he is not afraid to stand up for what is right. Sometimes, he says, he has to "play merry hell" with his fellow workers and with management. He has taken union responsibilities. Instead of being a clock watcher, he now considers that he has a job to do. And people are beginning to seek him out for all kinds of counsel. He still finds it hard to determine what are Christian judgments in the work situation, but he has taken responsibility for a "lay project" which draws about fifteen people into weekly meetings at the plant after work hours. He finds it natural to pray but does not attend the local church, simply receiving communion once a month in the cathedral.

From a similar mission, the South London Industrial Mission, comes the story of a maintenance fitter at a power station. He is also his local union's go-between with management. During a difficult strike he prayed often for wisdom and that justice would be done, yet he was not a churchgoer. When a missioner began to visit his power station he was surprised to find that he could let off steam about the church without giving offense. Now he is "key man" for the mission at the power station, which means that he is the mission's agent at that place. He has also decided to be confirmed into church membership. People come to him with their problems. "You have to be a doctor, a lawyer and a priest on this job," he protests. He finds that he needs to pray for help in tackling his responsibilities.

At Sheffield an active Methodist layman found that the Industrial Mission opened up a whole new side to his faith. He had taken his faith seriously but had not related it to his work world. He continues to be active in a "fellowship" within his Methodist chapel, but he does not feel successful in showing the other members how faith should relate to the whole of life. At work these others set a good example by not swearing, drinking, or gambling. But this man thinks such behavior only makes non-Christians feel uneasy or even act hypocritically around such a "good example."

For several years this Methodist has run a "lay project" as his approach to Christianity in the steel mill. Once a week he conducts a meeting during a meal break. On the average, fifteen people (in each of three rotating shifts) take their tea into the corner where the meeting is held. One person introduces the subject for the day, and, after the eating is finished, general discussion follows. Sometimes atheists participate. The subject may deal with a current social or political issue or with problems involving their work. Occasionally these meetings lead to some action to solve a problem. Progress is slow, but there is evidence of a changed work atmosphere in that department and others have expressed an interest in the objectives of the mission.[1]

In taking a fresh and radical approach to the modern generation the Evangelical Academies and the Sheffield Industrial Mission have attempted sustained penetration into

---

[1] These personal stories are drawn from Richard Taylor, *Christians in an Industrial Society* (London, SCM, 1961). Concerning the Sheffield Industrial Mission, see E. R. Wickham, *Church and People in an Industrial City* (London, Lutterworth, 1958).

common life situations. They have worked from within the public forum and the steel mill. These are creative experiments. But they have failed in one respect. This item of failure makes quite clear the sharp need for a lay ministry of salt.

The Call for Laymen

The leaders of these efforts have been mostly clergymen. And the laymen with whom they work have, for the most part, been unable to relate themselves to ordinary congregational life. Those whose Christian interest has been aroused within the steel plant or around an academy discussion find the local congregation too ingrown and too withdrawn from public issues. A great gulf remains unbridged.

In the early days of his Mission in Sheffield, Canon Wickham had made something of a break-through, he felt, in bringing a union official fully into the Mission. Later he was surprised to discover that that man had resigned from his union post, just assuming that to become an active churchman meant to stay out of union leadership.

Obviously, the call is for laymen, rooted in the resources of congregational life, to carry their saltness into the factories or other workplaces where they belong during long hours every week. Just as windows are part of the building, so salt becomes part of the soup. Only laymen can readily belong that way. Clergy remain a foreign element unless they give up their clerical role (which was the case with many of the famous worker-priests of France until the Vatican prohibited their movement).

The church's task of scattering and permeating belongs fundamentally to the ministry of laymen. They are the priests for the secular world. If the light image makes laymen ambassadors who bring something from beyond to bear upon this secular world, then the salt image makes laymen priests who are real parts of this secular world. They belong integrally to all facets of the transient, relative life of mankind and can fully represent it before its creator and redeemer. The church is dispersed salt in the persons of its laymen during their weekday activity.

One private-duty nurse in New York City who no longer has family responsibilities regularly commits her day to the Lord's keeping and in her work seeks out patients who are not Christians. As she nurses them back to health she quietly lives her Christian faith with them. Her faith is contagious enough that she has brought a number of her patients, mostly Jews, to a Christian commitment. The same method is recommended in the story of the railroad man who was converted to Christ and asked his pastor what to do. The pastor asked him about his daily work. "I'm an engineer." "Right," came the quick retort; "your first responsibility is the fireman."

Actually, that is the basic way in which the Gospel is proclaimed to man—by a kind of "good infection," as C. S. Lewis puts it. In most cases, carrying the Gospel to the world will have to be done in the close, everyday interaction of the Christian with the man next to him. It was one of Luther's keenest insights that the daily context of work, home, and play provides the occasion and the tools and the neighbor whereby one is called of God to love, to serve, and to gossip the Gospel. The layman's ministry of salt is to immerse himself and lose himself in that very context. Those characteristics which have been described as the Christian's peculiar dimension—his readiness to serve and his transparency—are now to be understood as the qualities which he contributes to the situation before him, the ingredients which he buries in the stew—a pinch of freedom and poise and integrity and alertness. Salt penetrates.

Other Qualities of Salt

But now a second point. Whereas light shows things for what they are, salt is an active agent in making things what they are supposed to be. Light reveals; salt redeems. As light, Christian laymen reveal what God is and what a Christ-lighted world looks like. As salt, these laymen are active agents of God's grace, entering into the world to make it what God intended it to be. As light, laymen point to Christ's presence in the world, interpreting events to show God at work in them. As salt, laymen respond to Christ's presence by seeking to fit their own actions into the actions of God as discerned both in the immediate happenings and in the long pull of history.

Salt preserves foods. Christians seek to preserve and nurture and enlarge all the goodness of God's creation. The Gospel itself cannot be stored up. "Truth cannot be pickled," declared Kaj Munk, Danish pastor-martyr who spoke out against the Nazis and was bullet-riddled for it. But the Gospel at work through Christians can help to form the brine that will pickle many other goods—materials, traditions, ideas, good will—which are likely to be needed in large supply. Paul tells Christians that they are to be transformed in order to prove "what is good and acceptable and perfect" (Rom. 12:2).

Salt can clean cuts and promote healing. Christians should be at the festering points in the world's many wounds, purging and promoting healing. Jacques Ellul has stated that the Christians' call is "to break the fatality which hangs over the world." There is a strong will to suicide in the world, he claims, and we must seek out the point where this suicidal desire is most active to apply God's will toward preservation at that very spot. Think of our juggling act with the H-bombs, for instance.

Salt adds zest and flavor to foods. So much of modern life is stale and flat; Christians have a responsibility to make it tangy and savory again. Take, for example, the ennui and boredom in the sex-saturation of so much contemporary literature. Christians have a duty to bring back the thrill and mystery, the romance and deep meaning of sexual love. Christians should be doing this both in their personal lives and in the way they write and talk about sexual relations.

Daily Work

But let us take this matter of the preserving and redeeming power of salty Christians and apply it to the world of daily work.

The Protestant Reformation made a tremendous impact upon medieval society at this very point. Men had carried out their daily duties as a burdensome, depressing necessity. Or they worked to further their own salvation and to shorten their fearful sojourn in purgatory. Over the centuries the belief had grown strong that if men were obedient to God's will as expressed by the church, they would eventually be admitted to heaven. Furthermore, it was felt that there were two ways of obeying God. The lesser way was that of obedience to the *commandments*, laws of the church which made their demands upon everybody, even upon common people as they pursued their ordinary tasks. If men failed here—and they did—they were expected to do special works—veneration of relics, pilgrimages, more severe fasting, payments to church charities—in order to get right with the church.

But the higher way, thought to offer a better hope of salvation, was that of obedience to the *counsels*. Priests, and particularly monks, were the ones who set themselves apart as specialists who walked this more earnest pathway. Their vows of poverty, chastity, and obedience to ecclesiastical superiors were intended to take them out of the distractions of property and business, of family life and of civic or governmental allegiances.

As a result, the monastery was considered a special gateway to heaven, while men who had families and common human tasks were in an uncertain position, distracted and lured from obedience by the cares and interests of this world. Inevitably the common life was viewed as degrading and rather ungodly. Church work was considered the real Christian activity.

Martin Luther boldly attacked all this. He denied that a man's effort and works had any value in making that man pleasing to God and acceptable in heaven. Only faith could do that, for Christ's sake.

The Christian does not work for his salvation. He works because he has been called by God into a heavenly kingdom and because he wishes to serve his neighbor out of gratitude to his heavenly Lord. Besides, God summons the Christian to serve men right where that Christian now finds himself, *in* and *through his present responsibilities* as a father, a citizen, a businessman. The monk has no special hold on heaven. In fact, he has likely fled from his God-given responsibilities, wrongly hoping to relieve his own soul's anxiety.

This is the Protestant doctrine of vocation or calling. The Reformers stressed that God calls men to be Christians in the midst of the circumstances and the duties that lie immediately at hand. New dignity was thereby given to humble occupations. The one test is the test of service to fellow men.

Of course, this Protestant sense of calling within ordinary occupations was often abused. The Protestant spirit of pious, energetic, and willing hard work was easily turned into something different, namely, the capitalistic spirit of competitive enterprise and profit making. Some people came to think that escape into daily tasks *is* their salvation; others decided that success in business shows God's blessing and promises a mansion in heaven. In America today researchers cannot find any clear difference between groups of Catholics and groups of Protestants in the way they approach their occupational life.

However, work attitudes stemming from religious convictions can make a difference. Protestant Switzerland and Catholic Italy provide a sharp contrast in the matters of housekeeping and daily work, though there is more than a divergent religious history to explain the difference. One American traveler calls Switzerland "a feast for the eyes," not only because of the magnificent mountains, but also because of "the lovely homes, the unbelievably tidy farms, the industrious and thrifty people." He notes that "such a little thing as a wood pile, for example, with every stick in perfect place, revealed the nature of these people."

"But what an eye-opener it was to cross the border into Italy," this observer adds. "At once, with no change in climate or soil particularly, there was a drastic change. Many buildings were in ill repair, weeds were abundant, crushing poverty was obvious. . . . The good stewardship in the lives of evangelical Christians is evident in Switzerland, where the Reformation did its sweeping work. In Italy, on the other hand . . . wealth is clutched by the Roman Church, but the people have lost, or never had, the sense of being workers with God even in an economic or social sense."

When laborers in Latin America, who have been part of the general Spanish-Catholic culture, are converted and join Protestant, "Evangelical" churches, their work attitudes change noticeably. Each tends to become more of a self-conscious, responsible individual with a reliable and morally earnest approach to his tasks.

It is increasingly hard for most modern Americans to relate one's Christian zeal to his occupation. Not many have the opportunity, or the greatness, to be a Florence Nightingale, stepping into a battlefield hospital filled with filth, infection, suffering, and sloppy care to create the modern nursing profession with its high ideals and with services both efficient and loving. Or, perhaps, in this day of vast industries and automated assembly-line production one should single out the contribution of George Romney. Romney led American Motors in the pioneering of compact cars. His company, together with foreign cars, thus provided the American public with a serviceable alternative to the big, high-powered, expensively tail-finned automobiles other companies were cynically pushing at the market. Surely it is both good business and in keeping with Christian service to market an effective and less expensive product. But how many of us make decisions that shape the course of the automobile industry?

For the general run of Christians, however, there is room for Christian action in the matter of our relationships with fellow workers. Here is the day-to-day fabric of work decisions for the ordinary citizen. As Robert Spike points out:

If you listen closely to the conversation of homeward bound commuters on an evening bus, you hear how much of the conversation is centered on what a bastard the foreman is, or how obnoxious Delores (who sits next to you in the row of thirty-two typing desks) is during coffee breaks. Or, on another level, there is the dreadful preoccupation with furnishing denoting status and hierarchy. Only a certain level of executive is entitled to a carpet on the floor of his office and only another level can presume to have a couch, and only the very top has a corner office with a view.[2]

Christians can make the office desk or the clerk's counter a contagion-center for the spread of God's gracious forgiveness among sinful men. Here is the railway porter who has become skilled in offering encouragement and spiritual help to people as he carries their bags in the station. There is

[2] Robert W. Spike, *To Be a Man*, pp. 40–41.

the hospital elevator man who quietly hums a hymn of faith
and courage as he takes patients up to the operating room.
A receptionist in an office building has learned to put faith
to work as she chats with some of the flowing human traffic.
A businessman maintains honestly cordial relations with a
number of employees not only because it is good personnel
practice but because his Christian interest in people brings
zest into every contact. A doctor returns home from a church
rally to lead a triumphant drive to abolish an abortion ring
in his town.

A certain minor government official to whom personal
problems are brought usually has to refer each matter and
start a file for what inevitably becomes a "case." This is a
dehumanizing system, as he realizes. But his Christian conviction causes him to declare that "it's *my* job to know the
person who needs help. It's *my* job to put up his case for
decision in such a way that considerations of personal significance are not overlooked."

Such salt within occupational life soon loses itself in the
vast and seething caldron that is workaday America. Certainly it is in short supply.

The Church's Concern for the Job

There is cause for rejoicing, then, that the past decade
has seen a rising tide of concern on the part of the churches
for relating faith to life on the job. A number of conference
centers like the Evangelical Academies have sprung up, seeking to train laymen for their Christian responsibilities in
their occupations. At the training center of the United
Church of Canada in Ontario, called Five Oaks, perhaps a
dozen weekend conferences annually will discuss "My Religion and My Job," bringing together farmers, editors,
nurses, dentists, office workers, civil employees, or lawyers.
These gatherings start with frank consideration of the prob-

lems—petty or mountainous—which are plaguing the participants in their work situations. Through lectures, Bible study, private and group discussion, and worship the conference wrestles with these issues.

Sometimes participants find specific answers for their perplexities. More often they find spiritual refreshment and the ability to face the tensions of their tasks. They gain insight for facing ethical dilemmas and they receive the encouragement of others in like circumstances. Above all they assess with new vigor the ultimate meaning of their work world. This is the process of cleansing the salt and shaking it out once more for its role in dispersion.

Such training does sometimes help to change work situations. A young fellow who had had a reputation as the life of rough parties both on and off the job found that a month's course at Five Oaks put its mark on his life. But he was afraid to face the gang on the job. On the first morning back to work he had to walk the full length of the hangar where his fellow workers were waiting for him. He was greeted with bantering and teasing remarks. Should he pass it all off with a joke? Finally he decided that this was a God-given opportunity. So he said something like this: "Look here, fellows. I've been at a place called Five Oaks, where we studied the faith, the Bible, how to understand people, and how the Church functions. It was the greatest month of my life." To his astonishment this announcement was received with something close to reverence. Here and there workers began to say, "Well, I'm an Anglican," or "I go to the United Church too." The young man finally concluded that "the Christian Church is the best underground movement in the world." But he helped to make it a matter of open action at his place of work.

There is a crying need for a still more penetrating kind of Christian service to the work world. One Christian who is experienced in labor union activity asserts that that movement badly needs what practicing Christians could contribute—thinking that is more than parochial, integrity in the lower levels of authority, a sense of responsibility that can overcome apathy. The same needs are evident within management, he adds; "I cannot think of a greater witness to the Christian faith than a Christian layman who is a first-class manager." There is no more salty Christian than the effective manager who can demonstrate the relationship of his faith to specific and difficult situations.

Kermit Eby, until his recent death a University of Chicago professor, was formerly for many years a labor organizer and then a union administrator. His background was that of the Mennonite-Brethren groups, and he carried the stubbornly upright, fiercely protesting sectarian spirit into his zeal for social justice and the cause of the workingman. Several times in his career he had been fired for taking a strong stand. Not that he would not compromise or work within an organization, but he believed that organizations and administrators should operate under certain fixed moral convictions.

For example, as an administrator he sought to keep open the channels of frank communication with his superiors and with those under his authority. He also believed in fair treatment of each individual. In *Protests of an Ex-Organization Man* (Boston, Beacon, 1961) he relates how a woman editor in his department of the CIO was summarily fired for having let out a verbal burst of resentment which was reported to the head man. Repeatedly Eby went to bat for her with his superiors, claiming that of all organizations a union should not fire without just cause and a hearing. His actions and their failure were the incident that forced Eby to leave the union organization into which he had poured so much conviction and lifeblood. It then became part of his mission in life to call for men and women who will carry their

Christian conviction into their participation in all their organizations.

Significant changes have come from the factory cells connected with the Evangelical Academies in Germany. These are little groups of Christian men and women who work at the same place and meet together to help each other do the Christian thing on the job. In one large factory the labor union had been dominated by a clique of Communists who cultivated attitudes of bitterness and hostility. Cells of Christians slowly permeated the union, broke the control of the Communists, and helped make that factory a better place to work.

During the great, week-long *Kirchentag* (Rally of the Church) at Essen in western Germany, management and trade-union leaders sat down together and discovered more common ground than they had imagined existed. A fresh approach was introduced into that labor situation. Some impending strikes were resolved through arbitration committees. One head of a large plant carefully revised his whole scheme of worker relations.

These are dramatic instances of what is happening more quietly in some other settings.

Essentially salt works in ways that are quiet and hidden. Salty laymen will usually blend into their surroundings. They will be lost or hidden to the eyes of any outside observer. Churchmen are made to be put in solution, forsaking their stored-up whiteness to take on the dull gray of the brine that mixes itself with anything that needs a saline solution. God's grace turns gray as it melts into God's earth.

Baptism, to be symbolically most vivid, should be into a muddy stream in the tug of an urgent current. If a Christian enters aggressively into a political party, his influence multiplies three hundredfold beyond that of the mere voter, but he must enter vigorously into the pressures, the power plays, the compromises and the flexible loyalties in the turbulent art and exacting science called politics. Obviously this involves the ready temptation to lose all saltness (Matt. 5:13) and simply conform, or, in our changed analogy, just swim with the current. That risk must be run, only keeping it within a dialectic rhythm that sends the Christian back to his resources repeatedly. "A man must be converted twice," it has been rightly asserted, "once from the natural man to the spiritual man, once from the spiritual man to the natural man!" Dietrich Bonhoeffer repeatedly insisted that to be a Christian does not mean to be religious, "a *homo religiosus*, but a man, pure and simple, just as Jesus was man." Laymen carry out a ministry of salt by being Christianly human. Salt redeems worldly things by losing itself in them.

To Fulfill the Creation

But perhaps this is the crucial characteristic of salt in representing the lay ministry: because it adds seasoning, it brings out the distinctive flavor in other things. Salt frees the egg taste in eggs. It makes cabbage taste like cabbage and meat taste like meat. Similarly the Gospel brings out the distinctive individuality, the particular God-intended purpose in other things. Under the freeing impact of the Gospel men become truly men and things find their proper use. Christians use things properly—music to be enjoyed, food to be eaten, work to be done well, possessions to be husbanded, people to be loved—all as intended by their maker. Christians also help other people to understand and use things properly.

As channels of the Gospel, Christians help other men to become fully men. As Harry DeWire has put it: "Within his life, the Christian is 'all men,' a world man, who gives not only himself, but shares with others something of themselves." Knowing in Christ the true measure of a man, Christians seek to draw all men toward mature manhood.

This redeeming process will help to draw out the distinctive personality which God has planted in each human being. It is a delicate matter of seasoning.

Such a redeeming process is also a matter of restoring creation. The salty Christian's action upon the world does not erase or ignore creation but helps to re-create, to bring sin-marred creation to its proper fulfillment. Gabriel Marcel asserted that "it is not God's will at all to be loved by us *against* the Creation, but rather glorified *through* the Creation and with the Creation as our starting point."[3] The abundant life which Jesus brought to men (John 10:10) included full participation in all of God's creation, rightly ordered and rightly lived (I Cor. 3:21-23). Redemption does not violate or override creation.

When Christians bring their "religion" into daily work and all the secular spheres, they do not interfere with the independence and inner secrets of these things—the laws of physics and of growth, the principles of technology and of human organization, the disciplined integrity of education and of the arts. The saltiness of Christians will be contributed to their work world first of all by complete competence and dedicated workmanship. The prominent churchman who as a contractor treats his employees well but builds shoddy houses stands condemned.

Tom Simpson, British research chemist, testifies to the relation of faith and his work in these words:

Although research is exciting, it also involves a great deal of monotony—it may, for example, be necessary to repeat experiments over and over again in order that we can be sure of the result. What a temptation there is to cut short that series of experiments in order to move on to a new, more exciting problem; and what a sinful waste of time this kind of inadequate research forces on to other investigators.

[3] Gabriel Marcel, *Etre et Avoir* (Paris, Aubier, 1935), p. 196, quoted in J. H. Oldham, *Life is Commitment* (New York, Harper, 1952), p. 99.

How short-sighted we are! The truth is that when we really accept that this world of work is God's world, and He requires of us our part, there grows a satisfaction with even the humdrum parts of a job. For God, who makes possible the most revolutionary scientific discoveries, does not value these more highly or use them more fully than less exciting work done in His name.[4]

The story is told of the African Christian, a baker by trade, who was an active evangelist and Bible teacher. One day he was confronted on a train by a woman who, upon learning he was a Christian, bluntly asked him what he was doing for Christ. "I bake, madam," he replied. She repeated her question more pointedly, but each time he replied only, "I bake, madam." The Christian does his daily work as a service to God by doing the very best job of which he is capable, because it is part of God's creation that people shall bake and produce and exchange and construct and clean. Luther asserted that the shoemaker fulfilled his calling by making good shoes—with a firm stitch and worthy leather—rather than by marking them with crosses or stuffing tracts into them. And the scrub woman acts like a Christian not by smiling incessantly nor by washing with cruciform strokes but by working competently with high standards of cleanliness. The point is that God wants people to have good shoes and clean living conditions. The famous cobbler was rightly translating the Gospel into good craftsmanship when he wanted to exclaim, as he pulled each stitch tight, "There, that will hold; I've put my religion into it." William Gowland asserts that bad craftsmanship "is really an expression of poverty in worship so far as the Christian layman is concerned."

Nelson Algren, contemporary literary figure, states that he has "no personal beef with the Deity" and continues: "All I say is that if your trade is a trumpet, blow it; if it's

[4] Quoted from a radio broadcast in *LLM Newsletter*, September–October 1962, p. 2.

painting, paint it; if it's poetry, write a poem with some poetry in it and let the God trade be. . . . People who are truly close to God walk the earth of man." To this a theologian adds, "May not artists learn here that their creativity must never be sold to venal—even piously venal—ends? For they serve the Creation through fidelity to the qualities of the materials with which they work."[5] Yves Congar, French Catholic theologian, focuses upon this idea in his very definition of laymen: "Lay people are Christians in the world, there to do God's work *in so far as it must be done in and through the work of the world.*"[6]

A Christian artist in Richmond, Indiana, has paid quite a price to fulfill his vocation without any compromise of his convictions as an artist for the sake of money. He earns his living by designing printed materials for colleges and churches. He does not hesitate to witness to his faith, occasionally speaking on Christian vocation. But he makes it clear that he is called first of all to be the best artist he can be without using his skill for any other purposes, even pious ones.

There is real danger in trying to turn creation into a pulpit for witnessing. The following lines by Edgar Frank reflect the sentimental willingness to push aside daily work itself as though it were not also the King's business:

> A man I know has made an altar of his factory bench,
> And one has turned the counter in his store
> Into a place of sacrifice and holy ministry.
> Another still has changed his office-desk
> Into a pulpit-desk, from which to speak and write,
> Transforming commonplace affairs
> Into the business of the King.[7]

---

[5] *The Pulpit,* September 1959, p. 11. The Algren quotation is there quoted from *The Reporter,* June 11, 1959.

[6] Yves M. J. Congar, *Lay People in the Church* (London, Geoffrey Chapman, 1959), trans. Donald Attwater, p. 16.

[7] *Stewardship Facts* (National Council of the Churches of Christ in U.S.A.), 1950, p. 54.

In our day, at least, the Christian style of life will be more salt than sugar. Fifty years ago American Protestants defined the Christian life as love and reduced love to sirup and sentiment and happy family life. Social Gospelers sought to carry family life out into society, expanding it to include business relations, politics and international affairs in one great harmony. And the Student Volunteer Movement sought to evangelize the world to Christianity in one generation. This loving imperialism, this Christianization of society, was an attempt to pour sugar over God's creation so that it would all be sweet. But the whole idea cloys and turns the modern stomach. God's creation is not all candy. Politics is different from family life. Not all men are ready to fall into our evangelistic honeypots. Today Christians can only hope to be a sprinkling of salt out in the world, helping these other areas of life to find their own distinctive natures, bringing justice into political life and the balance of power into world affairs, seasoning men toward their true manhood. It is not a time of sugar.

We may even have to rub salt into the world's deep and festering wounds. Such action may purge. Surely it will irritate. In fact, at nearly every spot in this world the presence of salty Christians will stir up the situation, revealing the deeper infection, perhaps starting the draining and healing process, most certainly provoking hostile resistance. Someone has likened the church to the gauze which prevents the wound of the world from closing prematurely. But the struggle of the Christian against evil is described more readily under the analogy of the soldier.

CHAPTER X

SOLDIER

The clergyman is often considered "shepherd of the flock," and the flock comprises the members of his congregation. This would classify all laymen as sheep. But sheep are notoriously dumb. They get easily confused and lost, they are passive and subservient, and if one sheep can be induced, even by a stranger, to do whatever the stranger wants him to do, the rest will follow. Sheep have no independence of decision and action. Besides, sheep exist primarily to be shorn by their shepherd at regular intervals. And such an outfit does not go anywhere. The sense of mission is missing. Sheep feed and grow wool and are clipped.

It is better to picture the layman as a soldier for Christ. Even the image of the suffering servant (see Chapter VII) could seem too passive and docile. Christians are militants —aggressively committed to an all-out concern for a cause much bigger than they are. It has been suggested that in the early days of Christianity the word "pagan" meant "civilian," to distinguish these non-Christians from those whose baptism had meant the taking of a military oath in the service of a new Master.

Paul once encouraged the Philippians with words that make an appropriate message for the modern Christian soldier: "Whatever happens, show yourselves citizens worthy of the good news of the Christ, so that . . . I may know that

you are standing firm with one spirit, one purpose, fighting
side by side for faith in the good news. Never for a moment
falter before your opponents, for your fearlessness will be a
sure sign for them of their coming destruction, but to you
it will be an omen, from God himself, of your deliverance"
(Phil. 1:27-28, American Translation).

Your Share of Suffering

Soldiers suffer, of course. In the New Testament Timothy
was told, "Take your share of suffering as a good soldier
of Christ Jesus" (II Tim. 2:3-4). There will be wounds. The
Christian soldier will bear upon his person the marks of his
campaigns—not ribbons but battle scars. The forces of
evil are not easily routed.

An insurance salesman in a city in western Maryland
lived for years at tension with his boss and office crowd.
His weekly participation in a Bible study group strengthened him to try to act like a Christian among daily work
associates whose spirit was quite different. There were conflicts. His boss urged him to work up to his potential, promising a rapid rise in the company. But this meant he should
not waste evenings with church people when he could be
making insurance contacts. And it was felt that his refusal
to use certain verbal gimmicks—not quite lies, not quite
the truth—cost him some policies. Several times the boss
angrily criticized this salesman for lack of loyalty to the
company.

One day friction brought a flare-up. The boss lashed out,
"For the love of Christ, either follow company policy or get
out of the business." The salesman startled himself by answering, "For the love of Christ, I will get out of the business." This decision to end a fifteen-year job gave him
a sense of freedom, but it meant economic crisis. After a precarious period of inadequate employment he got a job in

the furniture business. His income is much smaller. Plans for a new home had to be dropped, and there are no apparent resources for the college education of three children. Many people feel that he simply committed financial suicide. What he has done, both before he quit and in that courageous act, is to make Christian decisions in his daily work situation. It cost this man a great deal.

A shipyard worker in Glasgow, Scotland, had been brought into the church by members of the Iona Community (a Christian fellowship centering in Glasgow and the island of Iona and dedicated to church renewal and industrial mission). As a leader in his local union he had acquired a reputation for fair play. At one point a new work arrangement emerged, involving payments for piecework that would set a significant precedent within the whole industry. The management, hoping to avoid a dispute, asked this man to fix payments for this job. He agreed and worked out a pattern that was considered quite fair, so that the workers were doing very well. Then his union wrote that since the scheme was unconstitutional, it should terminate immediately. Sticking his neck out, he called a meeting of the men on the job, at which the vote went against the union's judgment. For this the man lost his credentials with the union despite thirty years of faithful service. He had to take a job with less pay. In fact, the incident helped to break his health so that he could no longer work. Though he is not bitter, he has had to pay a high price for carrying out his duties on the job according to his Christian convictions.

Battles and an Enemy

The image of the layman as a soldier emphasizes that there are battles to be fought and an enemy to be opposed. This world is not only God's creation and the habitat of laymen. It is also twisted and perverted by sin so that it becomes the domain of the enemy (I John 5:19, John 12: 31) and the battleground between the forces of evil, led by the devil, and the forces of redemption, led by Christ. Sometimes the New Testament even speaks as though the world were in itself evil, something for Christians to overcome (Eph. 2:2, I John 5:4–5).

Throughout this world a war is raging between God and the devil. The warfare centers in a man's heart and the issues of belief and unbelief, but it is fought throughout all of life. Christ is the rightful Lord of all this world (Col. 1:15 –20, II Cor. 4:5). This lordship is recognized where hearts are believing and in so far as social structures reflect the way God orders his creation. This lordship meets rebellion where hearts are unbelieving and where social structures reflect a demonic disorder.

Sometimes we are inclined to think that this is God's world and at other times we are inclined to think the devil has it in his grasp. The truth lies somewhere between. The best illustration is that which comes from the experience in World War II when men lived between D day and V-day. From the Christian standpoint D day is behind us, the first Easter. The beachhead is established. The crucial victory has been won by Christ Jesus, who took the form of a servant, became a man, and went to the cross and through death and now has been given the victory and highly exalted by God himself (Phil. 2:6–11, Heb. 2:14, Luke 10: 1–8). But it is not yet V-day. Not every knee bows before him as yet. In fact, the Usurper has many troops and still possesses many strongholds. We must penetrate these places, proclaiming the rightful Lordship of Christ. Thus we live between the time of Easter and the time of Christ's return in glory. Christ is Lord, but we must help to make this evident, to make it a fact as well as a promise. The tension here is well expressed in John Ellerton's hymn:

Thine *is* the loom, the forge, the mart,
The wealth of land and sea;
The worlds of science and of art,
Revealed and ruled by Thee.

Then *let us prove* our heavenly birth
In all we do and know:
And claim the kingdom of the earth
For Thee, and not thy foe.

It is clear, then, that the Christian will live at tension with his evironment and in conflict with much that goes on around him. Indeed the tension and struggle are within him as he wrestles against his own unbelief and sin. Paul speaks of a war within his own members (Rom. 7:2–3). He also points out that the Christian has godly weapons for this conflict (II Cor. 10:3–4) and describes the armor of God with which one may "stand against the wiles of the devil" (Eph. 6:10–17). Those characteristics which have been described as the peculiar dimension of the Christian now become weapons for his warfare.

However, the layman's ministry as soldier is primarily out in the world and his weapons are for struggle "against the principalities, against the powers, against the world rulers of this present darkness, against the spiritual hosts of wickedness" (Eph. 6:12). His purpose in life includes a mission of prophetic judgment upon the evils in society and the wrong doings of his own group. There should be an explosive quality about his presence in any situation. Helmut Thielicke has deplored the great number of "Christian duds who have burrowed themselves into the ground and think they have done their duty."

H. H. Dexter, in her book *What's Right with Race Relations* (Harper, 1958), points out that when the first Negro students were enrolled in the public school of Clay, Kentucky, in 1956, the white parents called a boycott of the school. One white mother, Mrs. Jordan Meazles, sent her children to school anyhow, because according to her religious convictions the others were not doing the right thing. Though she was ostracized, she persisted. When the Negro children were removed from the school, Mrs. Meazles continued her campaign. She wrote to the mayor and talked to her friends and to the mothers of children she knew. As a result of her sturdy actions there has been some progress and some change of attitudes.

It is not surprising that there are times when a Christian is forced to declare that "for the love of Christ, I will get out of the business." When the issue is clear-cut, that is the right decision despite the consequences. To remain in that job would mean that one was being "conformed to this world" (Rom. 12:2) instead of witnessing to the will of God.

To Stay or to Quit

Of course, there may be other alternatives, especially when one's service to a number of people hinges upon holding that position. It may become his Christian task to remain at that post as long as possible, maintaining the tension with his boss and associates, seeking to change their outlook and actions, patiently sticking to whatever Christian witness he can maintain in that situation. The salesman then tries to act "against the 'tilted' and 'loaded' policies of the company and carries on subversively honest activities among his fellow employees and customers." He would hope to behave "wisely (that is, diplomatically, carefully, intelligently, strategically) as a serpent and innocently (that is, with a single purpose to serve the will of God revealed in Jesus Christ) as a dove, in all things acting in compassion and love."[1]

[1] *Crossroads,* October 18, 1959, p. 58.

Herman Stuempfle, whose work has included the training of laymen for their Christian responsibilities on the job, tells the following essentially true story.[2]

"This is the break we've been waiting for," Frank Johnson shouted when he received the letter from "Conroy and Stapleton, Makers of Fine Furniture since 1913." The letter contained a job offer—plant manager, at a salary that made his present pay check look puny.

Frank and his wife Mary didn't have to "think it over," as the letter suggested. His income couldn't keep up with the demands of a growing family, his present job held no future. The new job meant moving to a new town, but, then, people were moving all the time in search of better opportunities. Mr. Conroy's letter, Frank and Mary agreed, was like an answer to prayer.

A year later they were thinking long second thoughts. "Conroy and Stapleton" was not what it appeared to be to an outsider. Behind the "fine furniture" for which the firm was noted was a shabby story of wages below subsistence level, poor working conditions and harsh personnel practices.

The workers had never been allowed to organize. Talks of a union were scotched by a few strategic dismissals. There were no official channels of communication between workers and owners. Frank Johnson soon found himself in the awkward and unwanted position of representing employees' grievances before the company officers.

It was also a risky position. Frank could sense Mr. Conroy's rising irritation each time he presented a worker's complaint or suggested ways of improving morale or safety.

But somehow he couldn't stay aloof. He knew that many of the grievances were justified. And he couldn't shake off a sense of guilt about administering policies in which he didn't believe.

[2] This story is reproduced here as it appeared in an article in *The Lutheran,* January 4, 1961, pp. 15–16.

The issue came to a head when he received a memo directing him to fire George Naylor. George Naylor, a lathe operator, had missed more days than he had worked over the past month. In every instance but one there had been a legitimate excuse.

But Frank knew that other factors were behind the memo. George Naylor was one of the most vocal critics of plant conditions. There was a rumor that he had been in touch with a union organizer. To management, he was a troublemaker and had to be dealt with.

Frank knew that this was the showdown for both himself and George Naylor. The easiest thing to do was to act as Mr. Conroy's hatchetman. Hiring and firing were part of the job he had contracted to do. To balk would mean a head-on collision.

That night Frank Johnson walked home with many questions on his mind. Was it fair to Mary and the children to risk their security? They would lose heavily if he had to move again.

He wasn't sure whether he could find other work quickly. Why should he be a martyr? After all, George Naylor would be fired no matter what stand he took.

Besides, he didn't really care for George personally. The man rubbed him the wrong way. And wasn't there some truth in James Conroy's repeated insistence that these people didn't *have* to work for him? If they didn't like what they found, why didn't they go somewhere else?

On the other hand, would not Frank's removal from the firm only make things worse for the workers? The owners would make sure the next plant manager was one hundred per cent on their side.

Frank Johnson was struck by the thought that most decisions are not between simple alternatives of right and wrong. Our choices seem more often between shades of gray. No matter which way he decided, somebody was going to be hurt.

Here was a man on the spot. His Christian faith could guide him and give him courage, but he had to make his own difficult decision. And either way he had to continue to live with the painful consequences of his actions.

In some ways life is an unceasing warfare for the Christian. He may easily find that faith in God brings heightened tensions with the world much more often than it brings peace of mind. The split experience of the layman (between church and world; see Chapter I) will always be an essential part of his role as a Christian. But, instead of a tragic gulf, it should be a fruitful tension between two phases in the rhythm of his week. When he worships he celebrates Christ's victory. When he is at his job and civic duties he knows that that victory is not yet fully realized and that he is enlisted to fight.

The Christian Army

Calling laymen soldiers points to a second truth about the lay ministry. Soldiers are part of a *corporate mission*. Laymen in their daily activities need to realize that they belong to an army, the army of Christ. We are troops—summoned under authority, disciplined and obedient, trained and ready for hardships. But the main point is that we are part of a corporate body with a task. "Onward Christian Soldiers" is a good Christian song (though someone comments that that song is usually sung as if it read "Onward Christian soldiers, marching in to snore!"). We are soldiers on the move. But let us not think of ourselves as in a medieval parade, proudly astride prancing steeds, decked out in flashing armor, with our righteousness unfurled before the world. The world does not want a parade of righteousness in our day. It needs fighters who will tackle its mountainous evils.

We ought rather to think of ourselves as a marine task force, a team of technically trained specialists, riding complex equipment, camouflaged and prepared to infiltrate the enemy and to strike suddenly and hard in an effort to fulfill some precise and difficult mission. Each man has his specialized role to play in an interdependent, highly co-ordinated movement.

What is the mission of the Christian task force? We must strike a telling blow against the devil and his forces of evil upon this earth. There is civil war abroad in the land. We Christians recognize the rightful king. It is our task to proclaim that he is king and to work for the success of his re-invasion.

Certainly we must mark the fact that the enemy possesses many strongholds. The devil's dictators have had their ultimate power broken, but they still fight furiously from many fortresses. It is up to the Christian layman to attack these enemy strongholds. That is, we must seek to alter the social structures of modern America, because evil is strongly entrenched in our institutions and social patterns.

Here is the weakest spot in the lay ministry of American Christianity. Laymen are unskilled and reluctant in tackling the massive evils imbedded in the organizations and corporations to which they belong. These huge power blocs and vast institutions shape our society and determine many of our personal habits. If these social forces are not what God would have them be, then our lives too are in fetters fashioned by the devil. Yet we have not begun to see our task as churchmen in this crucial area. Two examples will provide illustration.

A recent description of a Christian cell among advertising men states that the purposes of the group include fellowship each month, carrying the Gospel to their fellows in the advertising business, and giving their services to the publicity efforts of congregations. No concern is expressed for the advertising business itself. Yet, surely, in a society that is sick, the advertising world is itself both a distressing symptom and a contributing factor. What is desperately needed is a lot of Christians who, as workmen within the advertising profession, strive mightily to improve that whole business. The same could be said for most areas of American society.

At a recent meeting of the Columbus Group, which is an annual gathering of directors of lay training centers in North America, a Texas businessman sketched his personal experiences of the scandal of the Gospel as it confronts modern social problems. He told of his disappointment with the organized church, which he likened to the lighthouse rescue station which so concentrates upon improving the facilities for its membership that it will no longer undertake rescue missions because these would jeopardize the boats and dirty up the clubhouse. He admitted that he was caught in a sharp dilemma when he contrasted the defense budget of the United States with the Sermon on the Mount. He deplored the casual way in which men today accept the idea of obliteration warfare. He saw a new form of exploitation in the present economic pattern, which pays people good salaries and gives them leisure time in order to sell them more products which they do not need. He related how he has more than once run risks for himself and his family by stopping his car on lonely Texas highways to help hitchhikers or stranded motorists. When questioned about his work world, he admitted that, though he had talked in favor of unions, when his factory was actually organized by union people, he found it a difficult time of personal testing. Here was a sensitive Christian spirit. One could envision him as light and salt and suffering servant.

Yet this man could not fully symbolize the layman's ministry in the world. He did not tell about battles within the National Association of Manufacturers and the other economic and political institutions which shape society and color the milieu of his part of Texas. One did not sense a churchman aware of the corporate nature of the People of God and ready to wrestle with the entrenched powers and organizations of society.

It is true that in the area of race relations, where the issues seem to be more clearly drawn in many situations, there are heartening examples of corporate Christian action, though even here they are much more rare than they should be. Harriet Harmon Dexter in *What's Right with Race Relations* describes a number of them.

In 1948 the Southern Baptist Women's Union held its convention for four thousand white women in Memphis in southern Tennessee. A Chicago Negro, Mrs. Rosa Page Welch, was invited as guest soloist. She made every effort not to force the issue of race relations on this occasion. Her white hostesses were embarrassed, nonetheless, that she could not be given hotel accommodations, going into a Negro home instead. During the opening morning session Mrs. Welch was seated on the platform with other participants, but she was later informed by an unhappy committee chairman that the manager of the convention hall refused to allow her to sit on the platform again. The woman assured Mrs. Welch that the group was not going to allow that decision to stand. While the singer waited in her Memphis home until the next morning, leaders of the Baptist women negotiated with the manager and applied pressures. In the morning two haggard but triumphant women were able to announce to Mrs. Welch that she would be sitting on the platform with the participants and eating lunch with them as well. This firm action had ongoing consequences for the Southern Baptist Women's Union.

Less triumphant is the story of Koinonia Farm, a co-operative Christian community located near Americus, Georgia. From 1942 until 1956 Koinonia Farm had developed from 440 acres of run-down land into a thriving farm of more than twice that size, combining scientific methods with hard work to produce pecans, peanuts, corn, cotton, goats, cattle, hogs, and poultry. Essentially, however, it was a group of Christians under the leadership of Baptist clergyman Clarence Jordan, consisting of ten families and sixty individuals who lived and produced together, sharing property and a common life of work, of recreation, and of at least one meal a day. These people believed they lived by the New Testament pattern—hence the name Koinonia, which is the New Testament Greek word for fellowship and sharing. The unique feature of their fellowship was that they merged their economic life entirely into one co-operative enterprise.

But Koinonia Farm was and is an interracial brotherhood, and this is the feature which has become uppermost in the minds of its Georgia neighbors. Repeatedly, especially since 1956, the community has experienced hostility, harassment, and persecution. Mysterious explosions and gunfire from passing cars destroyed its roadside stand, much of its valuable special equipment, and a couple of buildings. Shots were fired at several members of the community. The members were denied loans and refused supplies. Insurance was canceled. Local merchants who did business with them were subject to reprisals. Some of the members were ejected from membership in local churches.

The Koinonia community has responded with nonviolent love. But continuing pressures have reduced its size considerably and made it more dependent upon the purchases of northern friends. Yet it remains a persistent corporate witness to a Christian fellowship that both transcends racial barriers and refuses to crumble under pressures.

Today some of the most significant battles are being waged over the inner city areas of many of the nation's great metropolitan centers. Only slowly are the churches learning that they must study city planning with care and plot their own strategy for the city as a whole, maintaining some inner city congregations with help from the outside. It is heartening, then, to see a bit of increased concern on the part of suburban church people for the church's mission to the inner city. This may mean that individuals who live in suburbs and hold church membership there contribute their time and talent for the neighborhood-help programs of an inner city congregation. Thus one man comes in on Mondays after work to encourage and help teen-agers with their school lessons, while his wife gives loving nurture to twenty children three mornings a week when she supervises a nursery at the same place.

Even better is the kind of group activity reported by the Inner City Protestant Parish of Cleveland. A suburban parish joined some of its youth with some from ICPP for a camping and canoeing trip in northern Canada. Fidelity Baptist Church, part of the ICPP, now offers an associate membership for those who belong to a suburban church but want to identify with inner city problems. One associate member quotes these words from a speech: "The world's battle lines run right through the heart of Cleveland." Husbands work with the Boy Scout troop. The wives help prepare a luncheon twice a week for fellowship and Bible study in a group that cuts across barriers of race and class. They help with unemployment surveys and the constant battle—against apathy and political indifference—to provide better public schools. They have provided transportation and a multitude of services large and small for a depressed and changing community that has staggering needs.

The layman's ministry in the world must undertake to alter the social fabric by seeking to change our mammoth institutions or we will be living in a fool's paradise and our warfare for Christ will be like Don Quixote's tilting at windmills.

No Lone Ranger

It is simply a matter of the way modern life takes shape. The day of the Lone Ranger is past. Whether for good or for evil, men live in vast collectivities. Power blocs shape our society. The spokesman for many people is frequently a powerful leader flanked by a corps of specialists. The rank and file select their president and turn over to him and his staff the task of making complex decisions. These mammoth institutions constantly clash—United Automobile Workers versus General Motors, or the farm bloc versus importers. Then each seeks its ends through the still more massive federal government, frequently by lobbying, and takes its cause to an amorphous public through mass communications— radio, TV, the printed page, and multimillion-dollar advertising campaigns. That man or group does most to mold America in thought, word, and deed who can deliver or withhold the most dollars for advertising, the most votes for a public figure, the most purchasers of a product, the largest attendance at an auditorium or stadium, and the best hearing in the precincts of Capitol and White House.

If Christians are to wield any influence, it will have to be within and through the vast institutions and the huge aggregations of power which compose our modern world. At the New Delhi Assembly of the World Council of Churches this fact was recognized, together with its companion fact: that the major Christian witness will be through laymen "who gain their livelihood in a secular vocation and are therefore fully immersed in the structures and powers of secular society."

From all this it follows that the day of Lone Ranger Christians is past. No longer can one carry through a Christian vocation on his own. There are exceptions, of course. A southern doctor who taught in a southern medical school accepted Negro girls into his classes for anesthetists and then took one with him into the operating room of the city hospital. Though he was advised not to repeat this, he brought her back until she was accepted and other Negro girls were given similar jobs. Even in this instance, however, where one man led out boldly, his efforts were being upheld by many others.

In most cases, certainly, some kind of concerted social action is required. For example, in Waverly, Iowa, in 1955 a Negro Air Force captain was about to move into an apartment when three other occupants objected. The Negro quietly found another place to live. But other tenants of the first building were unhappy about the rejection. They sent a letter to the newspaper, held a reception for the Negro family, and led in stirring up a wave of good will in Waverly for this incoming Negro couple.

Christians, combined with all men of the same temper, will tackle problems together. This applies whether it be work associates seeking change within an office or a factory, whether it be union men exerting pressure within the union and lawyers wielding influence within the bar association of a city or nation, or whether it be citizens moving toward wise laws and civic justice. Each layman venturing forth should know that he is supported by his fellow Christians. Even when the church is dispersed each member should be aware that he belongs to a corporate enterprise along with all other Christians near him. In Gideon's remarkable victory over the Midianites it is notable that his small army "stood every man in his place round about the camp" (Judg. 7:21).

In the *LLM Newsletter* for September–October 1962, Christina McDonald, headmistress of a British school, points out some of the difficulties and discouragements of the schoolteacher who struggles endlessly against time, against apathy and carelessness, against delinquency. But, she points out, with the eyes of faith the teacher faces her personal anxieties in a different perspective. She becomes aware of the pressures which underlie much of the difficult behavior of her pupils. "Nor," she adds, "does one struggle alone in the faith. I am constantly supported and strengthened by the faith of my colleagues." As an example of such encouragement she describes the teacher who brings to her headmistress the dull boy who has been so difficult to work with, exclaiming with shining eyes: "Look at what Johnny has managed today!" Together they take courage for their tasks.

In a youth group in an English city one of the girls told her friends that the following day at her work she would be asked to remove the foreign labels from certain products and to insert labels saying "Made in England." These young Christians discussed earnestly the problem this posed for her. They wanted to tell her to object to such dishonesty or to refuse to carry it out. But they knew this could mean loss of a job. So they dug into their own pockets and gave her a solid sum of money, promising her more if she should be fired until she could secure another job. The next day her employer was astonished at her firm stand and evidently favorably impressed by it. The point is that she was strengthened by her Christian group to act upon her convictions.

In the stress upon the corporate mission of the church, in which all laymen should be absorbed, one could liken the church to the broad ranges of a large-scale infantry attack. John Strube describes it in these words: "When the infantry division is in the attack every man and unit is dedicated to the support of every other man and unit in that division."

He goes on to describe how every specialty—artillery, engineers, transportation, medics—has its specific assignment in a battle, and how every unit, from the division and regiment on down, has its task of contributing to the common effort by closely interrelated action.

"This principle," Strube writes, "is carried on through the

companies, companies supporting companies, into platoons, platoons supporting platoons, and within the platoons, squads supporting squads. And then within the squads individual soldiers support other individuals. In this entire picture we see men giving themselves completely to serving others in the attempt to fulfill a mission."

In this analogy the clergy may well be the officers within the transportation, quartermaster, and commissary units. And organized church activities are the units which provide resources for the fighting. The rest of the division consists of laymen in their daily work.

The individual is called to particular assignments—perhaps many of them, perhaps one overriding goal in life—but always within the larger team purpose, the over-all summons and mission of the church. Each is called to use the gifts God has given him in behalf of the total undertaking.

At just this point purely congregational and purely denominational loyalties are a severe handicap. Nothing much will happen so long as one denomination stirs up concern for skid-row bums while another plugs for refugees, another for pacifism, and yet another for temperance without co-ordination and without common cause. And if a Christian's major loyalty is to a particular denominational label he will be slow to rally to the support of great Protestant or Christian principles, such as human freedom and justice and welfare. Under such conditions no real attack is mounted against some of the greatest social evils, for example, the rivalry for advancement and the conspicuous consumption of material goods.

At his daily work it is hard enough for a layman to know what it means to act like a Christian without asking how to act like a Lutheran or a Baptist! Nor does it make much sense ultimately to gather together Presbyterian doctors or Episcopalian nurses to face the tensions and issues of their professions. It will have to be through such co-operative organizations as the National Council of Churches that the organized church can provide corporate support for the laymen in their weekday struggles.

No Religious Imperialism

But once again a warning must be sounded. We are not talking about a religious imperialism that is bent upon establishing the dominance of church institutions and ideas over other areas of the common life. We are no longer in the day of Christian crusades, whether to abolish war or to establish prohibition or to evangelize a city. Nor can we think of the contemporary church as a well-fortressed bulwark of defense for modern civilization—against popery, secularism, vice, Communism—needing only occasional inner revival and some expansion of its power in society.

There is a significant place for the pronouncements of the organized church upon current social problems. And there is an important role for the church's representatives who express their judgments to the lawmakers. Christians, with the wise help of their organized church activities, should be among the citizenry who are best informed and most concerned about the burning public issues. When a broad consensus emerges among Christians on a political decision, that should find expression at the polls and in the halls of legislatures. The institutional church should be a fellowship that fosters decisive commitment concerning public policy. But the main impact of the Christian witness will not be made through the direct activities of the church organized as an assembly and an institution. It will be made through laymen who are dispersed and at work within the other groupings of society.

Today the Christian church is a scattered minority throughout the world with no home base to call "Christendom." America has become pluralistic, which means that different viewpoints or philosophies or world views must live together without the dominance of any one. For Christianity it is a day of encounters within society rather than of revivals or crusades.

The devil is the enemy; much of our civilization and many parts of our social structures are no man's land or at least uncertain and unmarked terrain. Christians can establish beachheads or bridgeheads as bases or provision posts. They can infiltrate and occupy ground and engage the enemy. They can send out task forces and mount limited attacks. But probably the illustration of a large-scale infantry attack is not the best picture for the Christian battles of today. We are an army of liberators, but not the kind that marches in consistent triumph toward a foreseeable V-day. The picture is rather that of the half-hidden, seemingly sporadic, persistent harassment of guerrilla warfare.

Some of us may find ourselves living within enemy-held territory, for example, within an inner city slum, at a certain level of management of a particular corporation, or behind an iron curtain. Then the biblical metaphors of the little flock and the sheep among wolves become appropriate. In the military analogy such Christians become the underground resistance movement. Their weapons and teamwork and strategy will be largely hidden. They'll have to use tactics of infiltration and subversion. They'll combine with all kinds of people who are intent upon the same immediate objective. Each will want to be closely but inconspicuously linked to fellow Christians who are located nearby. There may be cell meetings and a code, but there will be no flag waving and few pronouncements.

However, both a guerrilla army and a resistance movement need careful co-ordination and corporate strategy. Seemingly impregnable fortresses sometimes collapse because of the patiently hidden and well-planned tactics of an opposition that coupled inner resistance with outer harassment.

Besides, both guerrillas and an underground need leaders, supplies, training, and a supporting fellowship. If laymen are to man the battle stations, the organized church will have to back them up much better than it has.

How will such resources be provided? What will it mean for the structures of the institutional church if it is to prepare laymen for their mission and to point them toward the urgent tasks of their weekday ministry in the world? The answers are not clear. Nor are they easy. They may well threaten revolution. The next section seeks to suggest what new emphases and structures may actually be emerging for this purpose within the organized church in recent decades.

These features fall into two groups, just as front-line troops need resources and help of two kinds. For one thing, besides boot-camp training, they need frequent furloughs and opportunities to go behind the lines from time to time in order to rest and be refreshed, possibly to be regrouped and retrained. In the second place, soldiers need support and supplies and leadership right at the front during the fighting. Similarly the church needs to develop two kinds of supportive action: (1) for laymen in retreat, assembled within the church's structures, and (2) for laymen dispersed upon the battle lines. In both phases it will mean Christians acting together in organized ways.

Resources for His Ministry

CHAPTER XI

IN THE CONGREGATION

A German missionary who works among the Zulus of South Africa describes the Christian congregation in the light of a Zulu *kraal*, which is a hedge of thorns to protect cattle from danger. If a calf somehow pushes through the thicket, he explains, in search of fresh grass beyond, the mother may follow and eventually the whole herd could push through and scatter, soon to be destroyed by wild animals. Christians should not be tempted by apparently greener pastures, he feels, but should remain as the family circle of the congregation, staying safe in God's keeping within the hedge.

But tame animals—sheep or cows—simply do not make a good comparison for Christians.

Mollie Batten of William Temple College in England has a better illustration for a congregation. It is a company of paratroopers dropped behind enemy lines each Monday morning, only making its way back to the supply depot the following Sunday.

For most congregations today this picture of themselves would mean a radical reorientation of their life. The worship, the preaching, the education, the auxiliary programs would all take on an air of intense preparation. And the subject matter would all relate to the decisions and situations that await the troopers in the weekdays just ahead. There would be no room for the "bleacher Christian." Discipline would be rigorously maintained so that all troops would keep in shape. Functional cells would multiply—intent upon Bible study, ethics, prayer, the care of the sick, and personal help for each participant. People would band themselves together with those in the congregation who face similar assignments in the coming week. Retreats would multiply. The congregation would be eager to fit in with the planning and preparing of the larger regiment and the whole military unit so that its paratroopers are not left without support. Through desertion, shrinkage, or subdivision many congregations would be reduced in size to function with high morale as a meaningful fellowship.

Actually, most contemporary congregations would shudder to think of the losses they would sustain if they took seriously such a ministry in the world. They would consider themselves too green and raw and would ask for further training and seasoning before engaging the enemy. Or they would point to their substandard equipment and inadequate firepower. They would plead for time.

But the wisest strategy will call for immediate attack. Delay would simply lead to further delay and greater loss of nerve. Some kinds of seasoning take place best under actual fire. Only as Christian laymen mount the attack and engage the enemy will they turn to the resources of the organized church with a real sense of need and a surer instinct for the use of such resources.

The troops assembled at Valley Forge one winter were a rather ragtag, forlorn gathering of men. They were discouraged, low in morale, and wretchedly equipped. Their enemy was both well equipped and strongly entrenched. Some of the Continental Army had bloody feet and no shoes in freezing weather. The men sat about licking their wounds and complaining. Many were mustered out and many deserted so that their numbers shrank visibly.

This pretty well describes a typical congregation when it comes to fighting the Lord's battles out in the world of business and politics today.

Yet Washington's army quickly carried the battle to the enemy and won startling victories. Similarly, our ill prepared and hesitant congregations must adopt a strategy of attack, hurling themselves as reckless troops into the skirmishes and battles that confront them in the issues of this secular age. Then, and then only, will the life of the assembled congregation take on its proper air of earnest preparation, perhaps even an atmosphere of anguished searching.

What help should an organized congregation, given such a sense of need, provide for the layman's ministry in the world? Let us look briefly at four kinds of resources: leaders, corporate worship, study, disciplined fellowship.

Leaders

At Valley Forge there was the inspiring presence of George Washington! An army or congregation is no better than its leaders. Some of these emerge from the ranks and move directly onto the fighting front with the troops. The lay leaders of any congregation are crucial to its life—many of them taking responsible posts both within the organized church and within society. But there will also be commissioned officers with special training. These are the clergy. They too play a crucial role. They inspire, train, build morale and teamwork, find the best uses for the resources. To some extent they plot the strategy.

Actually, however, the clergy are the top officers only

for the assembled phase of the congregation's life. In the analogy of the infantry division they are the officers of the transportation, communication, quartermaster, commissary, medical and similar units. Organized church activities are the units which provide resources for the army. The fighting units of the division consist of laymen in their weekday existence.

However, the military analogy has its limits. The relation of clergy to laity is hardly the same as the commissioned officer's relation to men in the ranks. The clergyman has no superior status, and his authority is quite different. His role has been compared to that of the conductor of the orchestra or the manager of the baseball team. These suggestions rightly point out that it is laymen who do the actual playing while the clergyman directs. But they also imply too much direct control by the clergy. And it has already been noted that the example of shepherd and sheep —a good one for Christ and his followers—is a poor one for the clergyman, since he does not have lesser creatures as his charges. The difference is primarily one of function, since neither clergyman nor layman is more important for the total ministry. As Eugene Smith of the Methodist Board of Missions points out: "We think of the loyal layman in the congregation as being an *assistant pastor*. We forget the equally important relation of the pastor as an *assistant layman,* helping the laity in their ministry to the secular world."

It is better to return to the role of the Christian as servant and apply that to the clergyman. Dr. Smith states that the most fruitful role of the clergy is not that of ruling but that of "washing the feet of the saints." In John's Gospel (13:12–16) this act is the very symbol of ministry, given dignity by Christ himself. Smith concludes that clergymen should feel a new urgency for this high calling of washing the feet of the saints "who walk the dusty roads of the secular world, living there as Christians, the Church in the world!"[1]

Clergymen are both officers of troops and servants of servants. Just as rank-and-file soldiers need supply depots, so servants need services. If the organized church is the gas station/garage that keeps the cars on the road, then the clergy are the trusted mechanics and attendants. If the assembled church is the hospital turning out useful citizens, the clergy combine the roles of superintendent, doctor, technician, nurse, and aide. All these are but agents of the healing arts and the recuperative powers.

Perhaps the distinctive role of the pastor in our day is that of catalyst. When asked to characterize the pastor's task, John Casteel, professor at Union Seminary in New York, tells this legend. At his death an Arab chief willed that his possessions be divided among his three sons, with the eldest receiving one-half, the next one-third, and the youngest one-ninth. The inheritance consisted of seventeen horses. After endless wrangling over the way of dividing this inheritance, the brothers were about to come to blows when an old man appeared riding a bag-of-bones nag. After inquiring as to the trouble, the stranger proceeded to add his horse to the seventeen in the corral. Then he gave to the oldest son nine of the horses, to the next one six, and to the youngest two. All were satisfied. Whereupon the stranger mounted his sway-backed horse and rode away.

The most resourceful leaders in the modern congregation will lead from the middle. They will not be authoritarian or limelight leaders who remain constantly in front of the group. Nor will they lead from behind, manipulating the people and process. The wise clergyman will lead from the middle because his task is to help the people of a congre-

[1] *Occasional Bulletin* (New York, Missionary Research Library), February 20, 1960, pp. 5, 7.

gation to take up their own tasks instead of doing something for them.

This does not mean the kind of leadership that depends on majority vote or waits for the band wagon to form before leaping nimbly on top. The clergyman has, by reason of training and occupation, a special responsibility to relate his own group to the Christians of other places and other times. He not only expresses and guides the immediate congregation in its inner life but also represents to his fellow Christians the world-wide and two-thousand-year dimensions of the Christian community.

No secular illustration is adequate to describe the clergyman's role, because it emerges from the *Christian* community and involves *Christian* leadership. He directs a portion of the Christian Church, which is both a definable sociological structure and a unique spiritual reality. It would take at least another volume to describe the ministry of clergymen.

What needs to be emphasized here is that clergymen are a valuable resource for the layman's ministry. Laymen should be aware of that resource.

And clergymen should ready themselves for such service. They will have to think steadily beyond their own bailiwick of the organized church's programs. They will need a sensitive understanding of the secular world. It would be helpful if many clergymen could have a special insight and involvement in some segment of that world—as chaplain in the fire department, as an occasional summer employee in the factory, or as a careful student of medical ethics or merchandising procedures or one of the sciences, for example.

Above all, a primary task of the clergyman is that of listening intently to the experiences of his laymen in their many worlds. As lay people return again and again to the assembled congregation, they should be encouraged to tell of their trials and triumphs, their needs and opportunites. Clergymen, and the whole assembly, should listen carefully and patiently, simply in order to know what is actually happening in the rest of the world. As someone has pointed out, the training officer must listen to the troops from the front before he can help them by translating God's Word into a small-sector battle map. The clergyman and the layman must work in close co-operation, since their ministries are mutually intertwined. Part of their ministry to each other involves a dialogue, each listening and each speaking to the other from a complementary experience.

In reality the distinction between clergymen and laymen cannot be sharply drawn. Many laymen, employed by the organized church, live as much within that structure as do pastors. And all clergymen have at least some life in the world beyond—as family men, consumers, travelers, citizens, etc. There are not just two ministries but many, often overlapping. There are not just two kinds of churchmen but many, with frequent changes in roles.

Three traditional functions of clergymen have been briefly described at the end of Chapter III—pastor, teacher, and leader of worship. It is in these three ways that clergy provide resources for laymen. Yet all three well up from within the Christian community itself, from the gifts given to the whole church by the Holy Spirit. The main energies of the clergy and those of the laity flow in two different directions, but they rise from the same spring—what God has done in Christ—and they flow from the same pool—what the Holy Spirit is doing now through the corporate Christian fellowship. Let us look further at some of these resources as they can be made available in and through the congregation.

Corporate Worship

Private devotions and public worship are the central resources for any Christian. His existence is sustained by life with God, and his life with God is sustained by many acts of devotion, which find their fullest expression in the common worship of God in company with his fellow Christians. To be united with Christ is to be united with all Christians as branches of the same vine and limbs of the same body. This common source and this common purpose are nurtured and made vivid as Christians gather in one place to praise and thank God, to receive the gifts of his Spirit together, and to intercede for a needy world.

Fortunately, there is a strong movement afoot to revitalize corporate worship. Taking its rise in Europe, the Liturgical Movement of the twentieth century is world-wide among Protestants and Catholics. It has reached into many local congregations to bring new meaning and power into their worship life.

One thrust of the Liturgical Movement places emphasis upon the churchly or corporate or communal nature of public worship. Stress is put upon the fact that we do these thing *together* before God. Previously many Roman Catholics performed their own private acts of piety in the pew while the Mass was celebrated at the altar. And Protestants came to worship when it suited their taste, there to find themselves individually enriched and inspired, their minds and their sense of beauty stirred by a paid quartet or an eloquent pulpiteer. Now worshipers are encouraged to gather in one place as the whole family of God, receiving his blessings together and acting out their common experience of forgiveness and unity in Christ.

This emphasis upon the whole body of the faithful at worship leads to an equal stress upon the participation of each person in the whole service. He is to participate intelligently and with his whole being. He is to re-enact those great acts of the Bible, God's mighty deeds in the deliverance of Israel, in the prophets, and in the life and death and resurrection of Christ. The Negro spiritual asks, "Were you there when they crucified my Lord?" And the Christian an-

swers, "Yes, those days were the climax of my whole life
and have shaped my existence ever since." In worship he
joins others who make the same affirmation as they relive
those memorable days. In fact, those crucial events—calling
forth confession and sacrifice and forgiveness and thanksgiving—take place anew in the worship service through the
Holy Spirit. Each worshiper takes his part and knows that
he is part of a larger history and a broader fellowship.

Churches are built in more circular fashion, with the
altar near the center and the congregation seated on three
or four sides for greater intimacy in the setting of a family
meal. Modern art and architecture are used to tell the old
story in fresh ways. Agricultural terminology is balanced
by new litanies in the language of an industrial age, and the
archaic phrases of the days of King James give way to vivid
modern translations for Scripture and hymns. Many features
of the service—baptism, processional, offertory, preaching,
Lord's Supper—recover their dramatic qualities to appeal
beyond the intellect to the congregation's senses and emotions as well. Since we live in an age of endless discussion,
and since Christians always expect the Word to arouse a
response, dialogue sermons become popular, whereby two
preachers speak to the congregation in reply to each other.
All worshipers are expected to take part in their own language in the prayers and the whole liturgy. They may even
help to prepare the sermon (and themselves) by talking over
the theme with the pastor in a study group the preceding
week or by focusing upon the text in their Bible study.
Dramatic presentations can become true worship, as when a
group presents *Sign of Jonah* or a scene from *J.B.*, Archibald
MacLeish's contemporary play based on the book of Job.

To be sure, all these signs of vitality become a more ready
resource for the layman's ministry in the world when they
are connected quite clearly with daily life. Here too there
are many helpful trends and exciting experiments. Modern

worship at its best never loses its sense of awe at God's presence. But neither does it fail to tie that presence to quite mundane, weekday activities. Christ's incarnation was both a divine mystery and an earthy act. The Lord's Supper draws its pattern from the daily family meal. Preaching builds a bridge from God's Word into the immediate human situation. Worship is not only the re-enactment of our history—God's mighty acts in our behalf. It is equally an acting out of our daily routine—doing everyday things in the right way, that is, under the eyes of God and from the perspective of eternity.

If George MacLeod sees a parable in that change in St. Nicholas Church whereby the altar takes for its background the market place and river traffic (see the end of Chapter II above), he means that the bread on the altar should be obviously the same bread as that on the market. He means that the sacrament should have a direct effect upon the pressing, perplexing economic problem of distributing foodstuffs to supply a hungry world.

The clergymen of the Halton parish church in Leeds, England, go into homes to celebrate Holy Communion at six A.M. at the kitchen table. A few men drop in to participate and then to eat breakfast, using the same elements, before going to their work. Thus the sacrament is tied in with household routine. In congregations in industrial districts of Germany people receive the sacrament seated about the same table at which they take daily meals. Before passing the bread and wine, they talk about the happenings at the first Holy Supper. At one church in England a carpenter's bench is used as an altar. For the offertory procession a housewife brings some bread from her home, a church officer carries up the wine, and the money offerings are also brought to the altar/bench—offerings from the daily supplies and daily toil.

Congregational prayers can be filled with concrete refer-

ences to our weekday tasks and our myriad consuming
interests. Sicknesses can be caught up in intercession, often
by name and by specific ailment, held before the Lord with
intense petition for healing if it be God's will. In a congregation where the members take their common life quite seriously, announcement at the service may lead to a discussion
about the following week's duties, with a number of members
contributing. A bulletin which gives headings for each section of the service lists as the final one, preceding benediction and closing hymn, "We Depart to Serve." At another
church the choir sings the following benediction by Martin
Shaw:

> Go forth into the world in peace;
> be of good courage;
> hold fast that which is good;
> render to no man evil for evil;
> strengthen the faint-hearted;
> support the weak;
> help the afflicted;
> honour all men;
> Love and serve the Lord,
> rejoicing in the pow'r of the Holy Spirit.
> And the blessing of God Almighty, the Father,
> the Son, and the Holy Ghost be upon you,
> and remain with you for ever. Amen.[2]

On Labor Sunday at a church in Anderson, South
Carolina, carpenters' overalls, nurses' uniforms, mechanics'
jackets, as well as the "distinctive garb" of other professions
and trades, were worn as an expression of the sense of vocation within occupations and as a symbol of Christian concern
"for all who labor." In one English congregation the members
do not have a harvest festival but celebrate an industrial
Thanksgiving Day: the engineer lays down a shaft at the

[2] Martin Shaw, "A Blessing," an anthem published in the United States
by G. Schirmer, Inc. (New York, 1927); London: J. Curwen and Sons, Ltd.

altar, the miner a piece of coal, the textile worker a roll of cloth. Thus they give thanks for their jobs and the maintenance of their families.

In a Presbyterian congregation at Princeton, New Jersey, the pastor used a unique series of sermons to tie in daily work with worship. He preached on Christ's relation to five occupations—medicine, the law, homemaking, business, and teaching. About ten days before one of these sermons he invited members of the congregation within that occupation to meet with him so that he could "pick their brains." Midweek after the sermon was preached he gathered these same people and any others interested to discuss and criticize the sermon and to work out possible follow-up procedures.

Several congregations, particularly in small towns, have from time to time held a special worship service, bringing the needs and decisions of a particular profession before God and the congregation. Perhaps six months before the service for businessmen, to take one example, the pastor and a small group of businessmen begin to prepare. The whole congregation and all the town's businessmen are invited to the service itself. There businessmen first describe quite concretely their work situation, with its dilemmas and complexities, its hopes and fears. Then a businessman or the pastor will preach a sermon on the subject, a sermon prepared by the planning group. The service contains specific intercessions, with businessmen praying for their customers and the town's residents praying for their businessmen. In this manner a particular occupation is seen as a Christian vocation and an important community relationship is viewed in the biblical light.

Much of what is being suggested here finds illustration in the way of worship in the East Harlem Protestant Parish. This inner city parish, composed of several small congregations in storefronts and old buildings in an intensely crowded and depressed neighborhood of Negroes and Puerto Ricans, receives mission support from seven denominations. Its worship forms have emerged from more than a decade of experimentation in providing real Christian community amidst a tension-ridden, downtrodden folk. Its leaders think of their corporate worship as a gathering of Christ's soldiers after their dispersion on battle fronts.

The opening hymn is one of thanksgiving to God for the congregation's safe return. Then the worshipers confess their sins of the past week and receive pardon and all say the twenty-third Psalm as words of assurance. Next the clergyman comes down into the midst of the people and asks what has been happening in their world. There follows a period called "concerns of the church." A man will stand to talk about an important school meeting involving parents; another seeks signatures on a petition making a request to the police department; a woman points out the need to register soon in order to vote. There are reports and requests for prayer for individuals who are sick, or recently married, or in some trouble. Then the minister kneels at the table which serves as the altar and prays for these specific "concerns of the church."

The second phase of the service consists of Scripture-reading and the sermon. The clergyman moves directly from the reading to the preaching so that the connection will be obvious. His message is based on the biblical passage which has been studied during the past week in all the Bible study groups. Here are soldiers receiving perspective and revised orders for the coming days on the battlefield.

When communion follows—about twice a month—the setting is as close as possible to that of a family festival when the relatives gather for a great celebration. On Thursday of Holy Week there is a climactic re-enactment of the first Lord's Supper. Long tables take the place of the front pews. One of their clergy, George W. Webber, describes the occasion in the following words.

"In the early evening the congregation, including children, gather for a fellowship meal of bread—the long loaves of Italian bread, common to East Harlem—wine, and fish. We sing hymns spontaneously and talk during the meal. Following supper, one of the clergy simply standing at his place at the tables, preaches a brief sermon. The text is customarily the foot-washing passage and is used to speak about the servanthood of Christ. The minister reminds the congregation that the stole is also his only symbol of authority, that of a servant. Following the sermon, the congregation in groups of eight come forward and stand on the steps of the chancel while the clergy kneel down, and, using the end of the stole, wipe the shoes of each person. Then several of the elders receive the people's offering and bring it forward to the communion table, along with a loaf of bread and pitcher of wine from one of the supper tables. The whole congregation joins them in large circles around the table, just as a family might come to a banquet meal, and as Jesus sat around the table with his disciples. Then the words of institution are read, the elements are consecrated and the communion is celebrated, following as closely as possible the Biblical account. The elements are passed from hand to hand, with the people holding the bread until all have received and then eating together."[3]

At a regular Sunday service in East Harlem the worship concludes with the congregation repeating Jesus' words (Luke 4:18–19) which are termed "our Parish Purpose": "The Spirit of the Lord is upon me because he hath anointed me to preach the Gospel to the poor. He hath sent me to heal the brokenhearted, to preach deliverance to the captives and recovering of sight to the blind, to set at liberty those that are oppressed, to proclaim a year when men may find acceptance with the Lord. Amen."

[3] *Concept* (Geneva, World Council of Churches), March 1962, pp. 12–13.

Study

The Christian who is intent upon his ministry in the world will also be intent upon training himself for that role. In order to be light and salt, he will need to be intelligent about the faith that is within him. Actually the call of Christ should itself make him an eternal seeker, an eager student, one who is everlastingly curious. Therefore he has a right to expect the organized church to be a vital, topflight educational institution that will provide rich resources for an educated and informed lay ministry.

The church has often failed miserably in this responsibility. Even many of its devoted laymen have had no serious sense that they needed to learn more about the Christian faith. Not a few college graduates have been content with an eighth-grade understanding of Christianity. And religious publishing houses have often catered to a lowest common denominator of intelligence in producing Christian literature. In fact, American church life has had a scandalous history of organizing itself and undertaking programs without examining purposes or methods in the light of serious theology and the deeper meanings of God's Word. American Christianity has been remarkably untheological; this has been one of its most notorious weaknesses. Let each Christian cry out for his own personal growth at this very point, and then let him reach out for it!

As in worship, so here we have a fortunate and significant modern trend. From the deepest level of the church's learning, from its biblical scholars and master theologians, there has come in the last three decades a great resurgence of theological vitality. Throughout most circles of the church's life the study of theology, i.e., the knowledge of God and of his relation to man, has become both exciting and relevant in our day. At the heart of this movement is a biblical theology whose major themes reflect directly the main thrusts of the Bible. Some of these are set forth in Chapter III above. Stressing the mighty acts of God in history, as these are centrally recorded in the Bible, these major themes revolve around Christ and his church as the People of God. They emphasize the mission of Christ and this People for the world, which also belongs to Christ. Beyond a record of God's acts, the Bible is seen afresh as the Word of God, the instrument through which he speaks his will for us today. And Christian tradition—what the church has thought and done for two thousand years—becomes valuable resource for our decisions at this moment and place. Thus the church in modern America has taken a sharp turn toward interest in theology and toward bringing theology into the service of present practice.

Laymen are coming to share this enthusiasm in increasing numbers. There is a growing list of Lay Schools of Theology to meet the growing demand. They operate at a much higher intellectual level than the leadership training schools found annually in many communities. Usually they are connected with theological seminaries; the interseminary school at Berkeley, California, is one of the best known. Usually on one week night for ten weeks or for several concentrated weeks in summer, seminary professors teach to intent laymen the same subjects taught future clergymen, though there are adaptations to meet the needs and thinking of nonprofessionals. At least two such schools function in Washington, D.C., one having its office at Central Presbyterian Church and the other for many years drawing large groups of intellectuals and even skeptics to its challenging lectures at St. Albans Episcopal Church.

This educational ferment, obviously related to the whole burgeoning movement of adult education in America, has reached into only a small percentage of the nation's congregations. But it has often proved to be one facet of vital congregational renewal in those churches it has penetrated. The Montview Boulevard Presbyterian Church of Denver has honeycombed its large membership with dozens of study groups pursuing a variety of subjects to provide an alert and informed community of Christians in the congregation and city. Many other congregations are feeling the throb of new life as they do the same thing, often on a smaller scale. Sometimes serious study can take place in structured classes and within the conventional Sunday school or women's circle. More often such study emerges in new and informal groups in which the pattern and subject matter of study are chosen through the decisions of the participants.

What is studied? Nearly always the Bible is part of the study material. Often the participants address themselves primarily to the Bible itself. This can be a valuable resource for the layman's ministry, if the Bible is viewed not as history or literature primarily but as a potentially piercing message for the student. Someone has suggested that the Bible always be read as though it were a love letter just received and written in a foreign language: one will eagerly wrestle its message from it with the help of concentration and a language dictionary.

At a recent conference at the Evangelical Academy at Tutzing in southern Germany, a group of university scholars from many areas of study compared the methods of investigation used in various fields. There were lectures on the methods of the physicist and the political scientist. There was discussion of how the artist and the historian worked with their tools. Then a learned New Testament scholar spoke. He described his tools and procedures as the other specialists had done. He told about finding the earliest and best manuscripts, about using archaeological discoveries and knowledge of the thought world of New Testament times. He described how one mastered the meaning of a given passage by careful reference to the context of surrounding passages and careful translation of the words. He pictured a biblical scholar skilled in the use of his tools and entirely bent upon mastering his material.

But he had a surprise ending for his story. He said, in effect, that the procedure was successful and rewarding only when the seemingly inert materials suddenly came alive and themselves mastered the scholar. The end result of biblical study came when someone spoke compellingly through the materials to the scholar—indeed, spoke through the scholarly role to the man behind the scholar. The scholar has mastered the material only when God has mastered the scholar!

The Bible most readily becomes such an instrument of the Holy Spirit when it is addressed and studied out of a pressing sense of need. It serves most fruitfully when it is used as resource for the Christian's ministry. Historically there is good evidence that renewed life is given to the church when it gains a fresh understanding of the Bible's message. But usually this happens in a situation of agonizing self-appraisal or tremendously threatening circumstances. One of the thrilling stories to come out of World War II relates how the Reformed Church in the Netherlands responded to the occupation of that land by the German Nazis. That church was split into factions and spiritually sluggish, but it rose with new zeal to serve its nation at that time of severe crisis. Hendrik Kraemer, Dutch layman missionary and theologian, tells how he and a few others toured the church, shaking it from its lethargy by compelling leaders of opposing theological parties to sit together listening for the Bible's message. Then the Bible really spoke to Christians who had lost their mission in a world crying for their help.

Modern Americans may not face situations so obvious and compelling in their claim, though most of us as individuals encounter overwhelming crises at times. Actually, however, the committed Christian will frequently find himself drained and desperate for resources if he takes his ministry in daily life seriously. The church's study should be pointed toward meeting such need. This means that most classes or study groups should start from the facts of the immediate life involvement of the participants. It may mean we start by discussing daily life and its obvious problems. It may mean we read a modern novel or play which confronts us shockingly with the deeper realities of our lives. Arthur Miller's *Death of a Salesman* has often served this purpose. It should mean that we push on together into ethics and theology, seeking to relate these insights to the problems of our present situation. In the process we may also move into many other fields of study—psychology, sociology, literature, or economics. All this will be as formal or informal, as intellectual or down-to-earth as the participants choose. In any case it should be oriented both toward the Bible and toward life's concrete tasks. Successful study hinges on motivation and depends on the degree to which the student engages himself personally in the learning transaction.

It is quite possible for such intensive searching to take place when a congregation asks itself about its own purposes. If it studies its own neighborhood carefully, or participates with other congregations in a sociological study of the needs of a whole city, or asks whether it is doing any effective evangelism, the members may find certain complacent assumptions shattered and certain opportunities presented for renewal as individuals and as a Christian community.

The First Congregational Church in Amherst, Massachusetts, found currents of renewal through self-study. After many of the members had been pondering such books as Hendrik Kraemer's *A Theology of the Laity* and G. W. Webber's *God's Colony in Man's World,* the parish started to seek a clearer self-image. A committee worked on a report. Twenty-three neighborhood "colonies" (into which the seven hundred members had been previously divided) discussed and criticized the report. The document was revised and submitted to the annual church meeting for action. It is a remarkable report in its evaluation of the professional ministry of the congregation in the light of the ministry of every Christian and of the congregation as a whole. The report is still more significant for its effect upon that parish and the several hundred persons who helped shape the document.[4]

Probably the right kind of study as preparation for the ministry can more readily emerge when the participants have come together because of some concern in daily life. Thus mothers can fruitfully study and discuss Christian motherhood. A concerned group can undertake to study nuclear bombs and the international situation. Another can take up race relations and the home-town pattern. Those who have experienced a visitation evangelism can study how to witness at their daily work.

One of the best ways to cultivate the lay ministry is to gather people according to their occupations so that they may study together their common problems at their daily popular pattern, which the New Delhi Assembly of the work under the light of God's Word. This is an increasingly World Council of Churches recommended in order to help Christians to be "the people of God in their own particular context." Take busy doctors, for example. At a dinner party a young doctor complained that he was tired of being unable to take a stand on the many issues of medical ethics in which Roman Catholic doctors have clear-cut positions. Someone suggested that he form a study group with fellow doctors in his congregation. This was done, though some

---

[4] See *Union Seminary Quarterly Review*, March 1961, pp. 265ff.

members dropped out when faced with the demands for their time and their deep thinking (beyond easy generalities like "Be just and honest" and "Tell the truth when you can"). After months of meetings, the remaining doctors learned to understand each other, saw how theology provided perspectives for their work, and started to find some guidelines for their most pressing occupational issues.

In a Presbyterian church in Fort Wayne a small group of medics met regularly as a "dawn patrol" seven A.M. prayer group. Through their leadership there has developed an annual "Doctors' Seminar" for the fifty physicians of that congregation. On eight Sunday mornings during the winter a theme such as "Christ and Hippocrates" is discussed. Eight men write high-quality papers on subtopics and eight other men moderate the sessions. On the average about half the doctors attend a given meeting. There have also been weekend spiritual retreats following the series. Here are doctors who have laid hold of exciting resources for making the practice of medicine a Christian vocation. Many similar instances could be cited for other occupations. If the paint salesman who was asked to sell inferior paint (at the beginning of Chapter I) had belonged to such a group, he might have found encouragement and advice from his fellow salesmen.

Congregations can also bring study of the issues and interests of daily work into much of the programing of their organizations and auxiliaries. Sometimes special programs of this nature can be developed. In one Boston congregation an eight-day vocation institute was sponsored by young working people. On successive evenings lectures and discussions were held for ordinary workers in such fields as business, office work, laboratory and hospital services, communications, and library work. The program aroused enthusiasm and produced many insights.

Probing into what it means to be a Christian dairy

farmer proved absorbing to nine laymen of the Congregational Christian church of Emerald Grove, Wisconsin. First
monthly and then weekly meetings finally produced a
mimeographed report which reflected not only their expert
knowledge of dairy farming but also their earnest applica-
tion of their Christian faith to their daily work. Subsections
of the report dealt with the matter of land use, the farmer's
marketing practices, his relation to his community, to other
farmers, to other economic groups, to the government, and
to other nations.

There are many places in the regular continuing pattern
of programs within a congregation where daily work can
easily become the focus of attention. This is a natural theme
for the men's auxiliary. Many a man who has had nothing
to say in the organizational life of the church will find voice
and express convictions—maybe Christian, maybe not—
when his occupation comes up for discussion. And he has
feelings and ideas about other occupations as well. These
should be aired and then brought under the scrutiny of
biblical ideas.

One men's organization in a Lutheran church in Colum-
bia, South Carolina, spent a whole winter alternating between occupational panels of its own members and presen-
tation of the five programs in the "Living Right at Our
Work" kit. This latter, secured through the National Council of Churches, consisted of five filmstrips with records and
leader's guides to provoke discussion of the issues involved
in common work situations (such as truthtelling in selling a
kicking cow or the eager teacher whose extra afterhours
work antagonizes her associates). When two lawyers on
one panel told how they put together their daily tasks and
their faith, it helped some members present to overcome
their suspicion that all lawyers were virtually shysters. Several used-car salesmen (by a translation of the kicking-cow
illustration) also came in for some nearly hostile comment.

Nonetheless, these men came to a deeper appreciation of the problems each faced in his work world. And at least the panel participants were pushed toward a clearer understanding of their role as Christians.

However, the small committed group provides a better setting for the real searching together which can undergird the Christian's daily-life ministry. Too much of the programing of church organizations comes closer to entertainment than to serious study. Besides, the Christian needs more than increased understanding. He needs a deeply supportive fellowship. Here is a serious weakness in the organized activity of the churches.

Disciplined Fellowship

In the feeding of the five thousand, Jesus turned a crowd into a banquet.

This was unusual procedure, for leaders generally try to use crowds by lashing their pent-up emotions and by unleashing their power. Thus Robespierre used the mob to demand the guillotine. Hitler stirred it up to the bloodthirsty extermination of Jews. The American rabble-rouser urged it to a lynching. The Chief Priests raised the cry, "Crucify."

It is thrilling to belong to a crowd, and it is intoxicating when animal instincts become overpowering in the herd situation.

But Jesus produced a banquet. He broke the five thousand up into companies comfortably seated on the hillside and then he fed them. It's nice to belong to a banqueting company. In such a group one becomes more of an individual, with one's own tastes and characteristics. Fellowship is more personal, involving private ideas and feelings rather than mass emotions and actions. To break a crowd up into a banquet is to raise it to the level of human fellow-

ship, though that may also make the association more superficial, less stirring.

Groupings like these—both the miracle-seeking, thrill-
hunting multitude and the sociable assemblage of diners—
are typical of our modern age. People used to live in well-
defined communities, meeting their neighbors at work and
play, at worship and in the market place, coming to know
the same people in every aspect and activity of life. They
experienced actual community. But real neighborhoods are
rare in the huge, impersonal cities of today. Instead, we live
in masses of humanity—in subways, cafeterias, department
stores, office buildings, factories. Our minds are fitted into
the molds created by television, movies and magazines, until we are ready to respond to the same appeals, ready to
become a shouting crowd at the football game, the political
rally, or the revival meeting. Many of us need desperately to
belong, so that restless throngs are in the streets, seeking a
thrilling leader who will make them into a passionate mob.
Ours is a mass society.

With the passing of the neighborhood we have also multiplied our voluntary associations. Increased mobility allows
each of us to pursue his special interest in company with
those of like bent. There is fellowship in this—the fellowship of the bird watchers, the fellowship of dog breeders,
volleyball players, insurance salesmen, Luther Leaguers,
Future Farmers. And sociable dinners multiply. The club
and the banquet are the very marks of modern American
life.

Like Jesus by the Sea of Galilee, his modern followers
are beckoning the multitudes and feeding the thousands
in sociable companies. Sometimes the churches deal with
them as crowds in great revivals, huge rallies, or the
darkened Sunday-school theater. More typically we emphasize personal participation, we urge each one to join his
interest group within the congregation. Often he pursues

that to state conventions until he becomes an officer who thereby really belongs! In our organizations the contacts are superficial ones of pleasant acquaintances who are nice to each other and avoid conflicts. But if the younger women smoke and the older ones disapprove, the smokers sneak into the kitchen for ten minutes during circle meeting. And if there is divided opinion on steeple renovation, bitter factions easily develop. Bishop Berggrav of Norway found American churches good at contacting people but inclined to become mere clubs. And, certainly, of church suppers there is no end.

Do either rallies or suppers create actual community? Even Jesus failed to create *Christian* community that way. When the multitude came to him, says the sixth chapter of John's Gospel, the people were seeking miracles. And the miracle of the banquet did not satisfy them, for they quickly reverted to herd instincts. Jesus had to withdraw when he perceived "that they were about to come and take him by force to make him king." The banquet experience had proved a shallow one and now the crowd was ready for violence again.

It was the same story in Holy Week. The miracle-seeking multitude shouted "Hosanna" at first, but later in disappointment the people joined in the cry of "Crucify."

So today many of the people who throng in and out of our churches, shouting in our rallies and eating in our fellowship halls, do not find community, at least not community with *him*. Because they are trying to use him or because they find only the casual affability of many church socials, they wander on to something else or they criticize and help crucify.

Not that Jesus was defeated; he knew the answer lay with the disciples. Not crowds, nor banquets, but discipleship creates community that has meaning and power. In the rest of John's sixth chapter Jesus explained to those who remained what it takes really to belong. "I am the bread of life . . . if anyone eats of this bread, he will live." Not banqueting but participation in the Body of Christ makes community. And the chapter that started with crowds coming ended with many former disciples going: "After this many of his disciples drew back and no longer went about with him." Only twelve remained who believed (and one of them was to betray him).

Though he never ceased to minister to the multitude, Jesus found it necessary to define his movement, to sift the following in search for those who belonged. They turned out to be a few tested disciples who were willing to organize their lives and associations around allegiance to him. The salt and the light issued forth through them alone.

Perhaps we have come to a similar sifting time for his followers in American churches today. Hosts of people deeply need true community and are seeking it. They may even know that they are really seeking Jesus. However, too seldom do they find within our churches the true belonging and fulfillment that stem from allegiance to him. Too many never actually come to know the tested disciples in the midst of all our banquets and clubs. Lacking that, they even fail to discern the Body of Christ in the midst of Word and Sacraments. When they do come to know and discern and belong, it is usually within a purposeful and intent little group.

The best hope for restoring personal, disciplined Christian fellowship lies with the small group or "cell" movement within the churches. Cells are small supporting groups in which Christian fellowship takes on specific face-to-face meaning. They may be called house meetings or house churches or enabling groups or personal groups. They may easily lose their purpose and become routine or ingrown or factional. But they can be a rich resource for the ministering Christian by supplying a depth of fellowship unmatched elsewhere in his church or in his total experience. And they can help to "disturb complacent activists" so that they become aware of their deeper needs and their real mission. Above all, they often serve as the way in which Christ is present through his Holy Spirit with his followers, as was the case in the earliest church (Acts 2:46).

There is an encouraging contemporary trend toward this kind of "grouping small" within congregational life. The teamwork of an athletic team which really clicks provides a tremendous sense of solidarity and oneness, binding the members together. Laymen need this teamwork and experience in the parish. The cell is a fresh way to provide it.

The cell is also a vital modern way to experience "koinonia," the Greek word for Christian fellowship which means common participation in the spirit of Christ. Centrally God creates koinonia through his Word and the sacraments. In the congregation this involves corporate worship. But it frequently finds its specific meaning, its workshop, and its detailed patterning through the face-to-face "enabling" group.

Cells must be small, from five to fifteen people. This is because each member will want to know each other member as a whole person. Each should also come to commit himself to the others trustfully. There should be a mutuality and common concern for each other and a willingness to share in frank discussion which may involve matters of some intimacy and private anxiety. In such a situation men and women venture to shed their masks and poses and to experience the relief that comes from not having to pretend any more. In terms of Christian fellowship this means that they confess their sins to one another before God and receive God's forgiveness from one another. It also means that they seek reconciliation with each other and with all men.

Prayer will be an important activity of any cell. So will self-examination and the search for spiritual growth. Certainly most cells should also be study groups; in fact, such open fellowhip is the best context for the study which was described in the previous section.

But cells fail if they are limited to mutual aid and self-cultivation. An equally essential characteristic is a common concern for an area of service or ministry. Discussion and preparation and intercessory prayer and relevant action in some mutual interest are integral to cell life. The concern may be directed toward the ministry of the cell's members at their jobs. The group may center around a preoccupation with the sick of the parish or town. It may point toward social action—helping to set up playgrounds, nurseries, and youth centers; seeking to reduce pornography on news-stands; fostering interracial contacts; working with the courts in helping juvenile delinquents, etc. Of course, its common concerns may change from time to time. In fact, a cell is a very informal group that should be open in membership, ready to split when it grows too large, and ready to disband when it loses its purpose (after a few months or a few years). One of the real advantages of this kind of loose organization within the congregation is that it can spring into existence from the felt needs of a few members, without fitting some organizational chart or securing formal permission from a governing body, though the clergyman's approval and help would be important. In any case, the zeal of a good cell will be outgoing and its influence will flow far beyond its original membership. A few illustrations will clarify this point.

Sparked by the reading of the words "I was in prison and you came to me" in Matthew 25, one Canadian group volunteered to help rehabilitate a girl just being released from the local prison. They collected money and clothes for her. With considerable uncertainty some of them received her from the prison matron and took her into a restaurant to become acquainted and to plan. In an atmosphere of acceptance they were able to arrange for her to get a new hairdo and to stay in a member's home while a search for a job got under way. There were both high points and low ones in the days that followed, but it proved to be the beginning of a significant involvement.

On an entirely different level was the action of a band of French Catholic boys. These boys decided they should do something constructive in their own environment. Feeling how discouraging it must be for unattractive girls to sit on the side lines at the Saturday-night dances, they simply started dancing with these girls. They were pleased to see that their friends followed suit, and quite a change of atmosphere resulted for these girls and for those Saturday dances!

A middle-aged man who was battling with alcoholism found himself caught up in the group fellowship of the Church of the Covenant in Lynchburg, Virginia, and later testified to the way these people had kept faith and hope alive within him, risking themselves to rescue him from "the pit" and accepting him without censure. One is reminded of the similar role played by Alcoholics Anonymous, an organization of ex-alcoholics whose fellowship approaches in quality that of true Christian fellowship. Both the fellowship of Alcoholics Anonymous and Christian fellowship are concerned to support people who live in awareness of their many failings.

Christian cells also inspire many an individual member for a significant ministry in his own daily life. One woman in that same Lynchburg congregation is a schoolteacher whose joy and peace are reflected in her trust and understanding for her second-grade pupils. Her contagious spirit has caused her children to want to stay after school with her for additional activities, so that her new problem is that of getting them to go home at the proper time.

Another young schoolteacher, a church member and part of a cell in Michigan, tells of her emotional bankruptcy and her serious discipline problems with her fifth graders. One night, beset by a crisis, she went to a friend's home seeking help and, in her own words, "there and then I gave my life to God—really wanting to serve Him. After reviewing all the sins I could think of, I prayed that He would just take them and forgive me. It was a wonderful experience, something I'd never had before. When I came home that night I felt like I'd had an extra night's sleep. I was both exhilarated and relaxed.

"In the school situation I finally saw that most of the fault was in me and not in the youngsters. Now, with God's help, I am solving the discipline problems, striving to get the best out of each youngster in a loving but firm way. I'm enjoying my pupils a lot more.

"There have been tough things to deal with, lots of them. The way I was before I would have been frantic with worry over some of them. But now I'm just thankful to God for all He's done."[5]

In Washington, D.C., the Church of the Saviour is well known for the high level of the commitment of its members. Though the membership total is kept well under one hundred, each is expected to become seriously involved in a small group so that Christian fellowship will be fully personal. That congregation has an astonishing record of services to its community and beyond. And its cells often work transformations in their participants. As one member points out, "alcoholics have won mastery over themselves, drug addicts have been freed, a tough ex-sailor has been brought to a point of selfless devotion, a skeptical young scientist now preaches occasionally on Sunday mornings, a

---

[5] *Creating Christian Cells* (8 West 40th Street, New York 18, N.Y., Faith at Work, Inc., 1960), p. 16.

worldly young salesman spends his spare time working with wayward boys and shares his home with one of them."[6]

Mention must be made of one more important facet of the bands we describe. Obviously discipline is a significant part of any small group's life. Without costly commitment on the part of its members a cell cannot hope to serve the deep need for personal Christian fellowship and cannot hope to help its participants be leaven within their workaday world.

The word "discipline" is here used in two of its dictionary meanings, namely, "training that develops self-control, character, or orderliness and efficiency" and "the result of such training; self-control; orderly conduct." Every Christian, like every good athlete or artist, is in a discipline of training. He needs to develop "inner braces" to resist social pressures upon him. He needs to practice confessing, being forgiven and reconciled, becoming one who forgives and reconciles. And every cell, no matter how informal, must have its working rules, to which its members are committed —faithful attendance at regular meetings, some orderly procedures in the meetings, and full participation in all group activity. Though they are only flexible instruments, such agreements must be taken seriously by those who would actively belong.

Besides, vital cells will help their members shape disciplines that will be useful in the rest of their church life and in their daily routine. These may include such items as attendance at Sunday worship, daily Bible reading, family devotions, and an annual weekend retreat. These disciplines should go beyond the specifically religious, possibly to include some civil responsibility, a course of study, a planning of one's use of time and energy and money, or evaluation of the quality of one's personal relationships. Such commit-

<hr />

[6] *Spiritual Renewal through Personal Groups* (New York, Association, 1957), John L. Casteel, ed., p. 188.

ments become the subject for discussion, confession, and suggestion in group meetings. Some cells have even tackled an economic discipline together—for example, putting a certain percentage of their members' incomes into a common service project.

Congregational Self-Image

In an age of huddled masses and lonely individuals Christian community provides an attractive alternative for modern men. And organic participation in the Body of Christ is essential for those who would be servants and soldiers in Christ's name. It is encouraging to note that in theological discussion, in ecumenical contacts across denominational and national boundaries, and in much church activity there is a growing effort to rediscover what it means to be in the church. This volume has sought to spell out what it means in the layman's life. Now we must summarize what it should mean for the modern congregation. Often it will mean drastic reshaping for a congregation. At least three changes are needed in the congregation's picture of itself: (1) there must be a disciplined integrity of membership, (2) there must be a cellular structure of personal groups, and (3) there must be single-minded focus upon mission.

Prophetic voices are declaring that the greatest single need within American Protestantism is integrity of church membership. In our culture nearly everybody belongs or thinks he belongs to a church. Many Protestant churches are easier to join than the Rotary Club. And it's much easier to stay on the rolls. Parents are insulted when the pastor suggests that they should be church attenders before having their child baptized. One pastor claimed that if he only had adequate parking space on Sunday morning his membership would increase by a thousand in six months. Many of the people who sign up, and even many of those who worship often, though they give out all kinds of information on a government census, would feel their "privacy" was shockingly invaded if a pastor or other concerned Christian were to inquire into their budgetary habits or their personal moral practices or even their spiritual health. Such shallow acceptance makes the fellowship meaningless because its fabric is composed of all kinds of secular purposes with the Holy Spirit very difficult to find in it.

This is a matter of discipline, which belongs to the life of the whole congregation as well as to the life of the small group. There are no formless, jellyfish Christians. Granted that there are many weak Christians, yet there is no excuse for the complacent refusal to place oneself in the way of getting help. Though the Continental Army was quite woebegone, Washington brought in Baron von Steuben, who drilled this mob into an army that won victories. In the Christian army those who refuse discipline will turn out to be misfits who will eliminate themselves from the ranks. This does not put such people beyond the concern of the congregation; it simply indicates that they have not yet been won.

To refuse such an effort to "mark the boundaries" under the excuse that God's grace is freely outpoured is to treat God as though he were a kindly grandfather who closes his eyes to the churlish or wayward acts of his grandchildren. This is what Dietrich Bonhoeffer, German theologian martyred by the Nazis, called cheap grace. His words in *The Cost of Discipleship* are a stinging indictment of much modern church life. "Cheap grace is the deadly enemy of our church," he claims, adding that "we are fighting today for costly grace." Then he explains:

Cheap grace means grace sold on the market like cheap-jack's wares. The sacraments, the forgiveness of sin, and the consolations of religion are thrown away at cut prices. Grace is represented as the Church's inexhaustible treasury, from which she showers blessings with generous hands, without asking questions or fixing limits. Grace without price, grace without cost! The essence of grace, we suppose, is that the account has been paid in advance; and, because it has been paid, everything can be had for nothing . . .

According to this German Lutheran, people demand cheap grace because they have given only intellectual assent to doctrine instead of life commitment to the living God. He adds:

Cheap grace means the justification of sin without the justification of the sinner. Grace alone does everything, they say, and so everything can remain as it was before. "All for sin could not atone." . . . Well, then, let the Christian live like the rest of the world, let him model himself on the world's standards in every sphere of life, and not presumptuously aspire to live a different life under grace from his old life under sin. . . .

Cheap grace is the preaching of forgiveness without requiring repentance, baptism without Church discipline, Communion without confession, absolution without contrition. Cheap grace is grace without discipleship, grace without the Cross, grace without Jesus Christ, living and incarnate.

Bonhoeffer goes on to speak of the true grace of God, which is costly:

Costly grace is the treasure hidden in the field; for the sake of it a man will gladly go and sell all that he has. It is the pearl of great price to buy which the merchant will sell all his goods. It is the kingly rule of Christ, for whose sake a man will pluck out the eye which causes him to stumble, it is the call of Jesus Christ at which the disciple leaves his nets and follows Him.[7]

Standards for church membership will have to be raised. This will be done in different ways by the various branches

[7] *The Cost of Discipleship* (New York, Macmillan, 1957), R. H. Fuller, ed., pp. 37–39.

of American Protestantism. In most cases it should mean a higher level of instruction before adult membership and a greater degree of commitment to ongoing study and to various forms of concrete support and participation. It will mean that quite a few applicants for membership will be turned down for the time being. It may mean that others will have to be brought to a personal repentance and confession before receiving the sacraments.

Scholars have distinguished three levels or concentric circles in the idea of a parish. The broadest circle includes all the people of a particular geographic area in the sum total of their lives. This is the field of immediate mission and responsibility for the parish. The second circle consists of all who belong on the rolls of the organized congregation or have any specific tie with it. This is the nominal membership. The third circle is the "inner essence" or "the militants" of the parish, namely, that concerned group at the heart of the congregation who have committed themselves to serving God through that congregation and in that parish.

Our congregations have usually defined themselves in terms of the second level, the nominal membership. No matter how the membership rolls are actually arranged, what is needed is that the congregation shall understand itself in terms of the first and the third levels. The first level is its field of mission and the third is its disciplined, task-force team. Those in between will have to fall one way or the other. They will themselves accept the discipline or they will reject it.

This distinction is best drawn through a second self-image. Let the congregation's inner core be defined in terms of a honeycomb of cells. Those who cannot find their way into that kind of fellowship put themselves into the field of mission instead of within the driving force for mission. There is an Episcopal church in Texas which requires as part of its membership covenant the participation in a witnessing

group. Both the previously mentioned Church of the Covenant in Lynchburg and the Church of the Saviour in Washington make this a part of the discipline for each member.

Do not misunderstand. Word and Sacraments—preaching, Baptism, Lord's Supper, and corporate worship—remain
the central resources of the church. They also remain the
inner marks of the church. But, as befits the contemporary
church, the small groups give Christian fellowship face-to-
face meaning for participants. In the ancient church it was
the large household, in the Middle Ages the monastery, in
the Post-Reformation era the family, in the nineteenth century congregational activities.[8] Today it is the cell which
forms the Christian workshop. The family, for example, will
not naturally provide face-to-face Christian fellowship unless
it consciously tries to do so; then it will become a cell.

The third change of image is that of focusing upon mission. Here we return to the picture of the paratroopers. In
the Apostles' Creed the church is defined as the communion
of saints, i.e., the fellowship of sinners who are laid hold of
by the Holy Spirit. We ought also to think of the church
as the communion of the sent, i.e., the fellowship of those
laid hold of by a mission.

It may well be tough going for congregations that accept
these three images for their life—discipline, cellular structure, and mission. From its beginning in 1954 the Church
of the Covenant in Lynchburg grew to only fifteen members
by 1961. In a large congregation in New Jersey the two
clergy and the governing council committed themselves to
such purposes. The one clergyman gave full time to a
venture in serious adult education, preparing for the layman's
ministry in the world. Much of the membership remained
lukewarm, and statistics of finances and attendance sagged.
More devastating, however, was the clash between this ex-

---

[8] This idea is developed in T. Ralph Morton, *Community of Faith* (New
York, Association, 1954).

periment and the grinding inertia of the machinery by which the congregation functioned as an institution and as part of a larger denominational institution.

A more detailed illustration will indicate that a congregation can conform to these three images if it will pay the price. In the *Union Seminary Quarterly Review,* March 1961, the Rev. William H. Hollister describes the life of his suburban mission congregation, Christ Church Presbyterian, in Burlington, Vermont. First he describes as "Suburban Blocks" the peculiar pressures of a beginning mission in a suburb—the desire to cater to children, the involvement in merely leisure-time activities, the urge to build a building that will please the neighborhood, the need to bring many people in quickly without sifting motives, the pressure from the denomination's mission board that this mission be a "success" and become financially independent in a hurry.

Originally (1955) those interested in membership entered into one of seven neighborhood discussion groups. For six months these groups met biweekly to consider what church membership means and what would be the purpose of a congregation in this community. After the church organized (in 1956) it was decided, after heated debate, that for the sake of integrity of membership all those who subsequently seek to join would be asked to take up a similar lengthy period of study in a membership class. This has meant slow numerical growth. When new members join the congregation they are asked to write out their reasons for doing this and how they plan to continue to grow in faith as members. Adult study groups are an important part of the church's life and the level of study is demanding.

Because of their corporate commitment and their effort to think things through together, the laymen of this congregation came gradually to realize that they had a mission which meant involvement in the city's life in Christ's behalf. This has taken a variety of forms. One study group has undertaken to visit prisoners in the local jail each week. These members are involved in counseling those inmates and are helping them maintain the right contacts with the outside world.

A group of students decided they had a responsibility to fellow students at the University of Vermont. On campus these students set up an old carriage house as "The Barn," providing atmosphere, coffee, modern jazz and poetry. Thus they created the setting for serious dialogue between various viewpoints represented on campus. And they play the servant role as question raisers and stimulators.

Out of concern for the occupational world this congregation is looking toward the formation of groups of engineers, homemakers, industrial workers, doctors and nurses, salemen, and commercial employees. Leadership in this direction has come from an engineer who is wondering about the value of his work in the making of machine guns. This program is also a deliberate effort to overcome the distance separating a congregation in a residential suburb from the decision-making life of its members at their daily tasks.

Another member of the congregation has rented a second-floor shop in a business district of the city as a restaurant and coffeehouse in which there is to be opportunity for dialogue between differing viewpoints and discussion of the issues in modern culture and society. This is a business venture, but it has the official encouragement of the congregation and is intended as a service in the name of the Christian faith.

Of course, there are tensions within the membership of this congregation. There could be no experimental Christian spirit without tension. The church facilities remained (in 1961) a renovated TV shop. In place of the usual straining of every effort in a building campaign, this fellowship has chosen to give priority to its mission within its suburb and city.

We conclude, then, that for the layman who would fulfill his ministry in the world his congregation provides the basic resources, though many a congregation needs drastically to reshape itself to fulfill that purpose.

Yet there are ways of helping which lie beyond the congregation. Soldiers not only need to go behind the lines for training and refreshment but also need supplies and help right at their battle stations. So laymen need resources and fellowship in their scattered existences on many fronts of daily life. There is a call today for new forms of the church that will move closer to the daily life of many laymen.

CHAPTER XII

BEYOND THE CONGREGATION

When David Frank describes the Business Practice Seminars
of the Laymen's Movement for a Christian World, he im-
agines three executives and the hard questions they'd face
if they attended such a weekend conference at the organization's Wainwright House in Rye, New York. Taken from that
Movement's *Review,* these three descriptions follow.[1]

Bob Black has a good job. He does everything his boss
expects of him, but not much more. Black's goal in business is to survive. He never sticks his neck out. He thinks he
has enough to do running his department without looking
around for more headaches.

When a really tough decision is being made in the front
office, Black's opinion is seldom invited. And when Black is
called on to carry out policies that he thinks may not be
entirely aboveboard, as happens now and then, he keeps his
questions to himself. "It's their company; I just work here,"
he reflects.

Since somebody else makes the policies, he is not troubled
about the ethics of business situations. They have no real
meaning to him.

If you were to ask Black to a Laymen's Movement Busi-

[1] *The Laymen's Movement Review,* November–December 1961, pp. 6–7.

ness Practice Seminar, he might wonder, "Why me?" But the ideas behind the seminar program suggest some hard questions for men like Bob Black:

If you don't find yourself up against moral dilemmas in your business, is it because you prefer to avoid them? Have you failed yourself—and your employer—by not speaking up? Are you as competent as you should be?

George White happens to be deeply dedicated to his business. Unlike Bob Black, he lives it and breathes it. He creates. He is a risk taker, and he is smart enough to make most of his risks pay off.

White is not necessarily out to make a fast buck. He wants to stay in business. He gets many satisfactions from it. He also wants to be a good provider for his family.

His goal is "to make the business work." If that means "ethical conduct" in order to achieve some objective with the boss, with the customer or with the labor union, he is happy to oblige. On the other hand, White thinks he has been around long enough to know when to pull a fast one— when he can be sure he will get away with it. "What works is good works" sums up White's moral code.

The Business Practice Seminar idea poses these questions for the George Whites of the business world:

If you could have arrived where you are without any fast ones— especially the ones where you got caught—would you do what you did all over again? Is your way something you could make a speech about at the Moscow trade fair?

Bill Gray is not only fully dedicated to his work but also competent and a man of integrity. As a result he is a magnet for one tough business decision after another.

As Gray climbs the management ladder, his problems get tougher and more complex. Each decision, it seems, becomes a moral choice, and the virtue of simple honesty is only a starting point, for no matter what Gray decides, someone is probably going to get hurt.

Gray wants and looks for all the help he can get. He wishes every man in his organization had a little less brilliance and a little more moral fiber. He does not know where to turn for help. So he is perhaps the most desperate businessman of all.

Thus, the hard questions the seminar program puts to the Bill Grays are these:

Are you getting all the help you need to strengthen your own inner resources and those of your people? If this is one of the biggest problems in your business, what are you doing about it —personally?

Since 1954 the Laymen's Movement has sponsored about a half dozen seminars each year, bringing together for a weekend about twenty businessmen to discuss the issues and the fundamental values involved in their business practices. An outstanding person from the business world and a theological-spiritual resource person provide leadership. Such a facing of issues together often has a profound effect upon participants. One oil-company executive returned home to alter radically part of a contract with a foreign government. Usually the effects are much less dramatic and quite difficult to measure.

There is much ferment and uneasiness concerning business ethics in modern America. This is caused not so much by certain headline-catching cases of flagrant corruption but rather because a number of responsible businessmen find themselves making complex decisions that directly affect many lives. These men know they need help. The Harvard Graduate School of Business Administration and many large corporations are studying the situation and providing ethical education for executives and others. One clergyman organized seminars in business ethics in a special car on a commuter train to New York City. Enthusiasm greeted the suggestion of Chief Justice Warren of the Supreme Court that there be formed a new profession of ethical counselors for large businesses, its members to have standing comparable to that of corporation lawyers. It is reported that the idea of regular meetings of a small group of businessmen with a clergyman is being tried out by a number of Catholic Employers and Managers Study Groups. A growing literature on ethics and business reflects the same interest.

This ferment is much wider than the business world and suggests that many people throughout our society are open to real help in ethics and "spiritual values" at the decision points in daily life. Probably the popular "religious revival" of the 1950s is best understood as an expression of this search.

To meet this value vacuum there has emerged in the last two decades a significant movement called the "Lay Renaissance." In Europe this movement has still-deeper roots than in America, emerging from the chaos and destruction, the agony and soul-searching that have accompanied the wars and dictators of that continent. On that side of the Atlantic the renaissance finds expression in huge rallies such as the German Kirchentag and the growing number of lay conference centers, called Evangelical Academies in Germany. There are perhaps seventy such lay centers in Europe and a scattering throughout Africa and Asia. Central leadership for the conference center phase of the lay renaissance has been given by the Ecumenical Institute at Bossey, near Geneva, and the Department on the Laity of the World Council of Churches.

In America there are about two dozen conference centers for lay training. Since American Christians have not gone through the same experiences of shock and renewal as have some Europeans, it is harder to distinguish a real renaissance from much of the business-as-usual activism which typifies American Protestantism. Nonetheless, one can point to such interdenominational fellowship as Yokefellows, the Disciplined Order of Christ, International Christian Leadership and the Laymen's Movement for a Christian World. Roman Catholics have comparable organizations in the Jocists and the Christophers. Some of the denominational men's work programs and some of the new ventures in evangelism are also worthy of mention in this connection.

Actually this whole book has grown out of the thinking of the lay renaissance and many of the experiments and illustrations here described belong to that movement. The central theme of this volume, namely, the ministry of laymen in the world, could be called one of the two main thrusts of the lay renaissance. The other main idea is that the church must move out into the structures of modern society to serve those structures in Christ's name and to touch lives that are now quite remote from the church's influence. Both thrusts mean a recovery of the central significance of the church's dedicated laymen for its life and its mission in the world.

In Europe the participants in lay center activities have often held aloof from congregations. This is not so true in America, partly because the gap between these two forms of the Christian church—lay center and congregation—has not been so great. Yet the lay renaissance has developed largely through new forms that lie beyond the congregation —with the notable exception of parishes such as those described in the previous chapter.

There is an obvious reason why congregations cannot fulfill the purposes of the lay renaissance. It stems from the sociological fact that modern Americans no longer live their lives and form their personal associations within the confines of a local neighborhood. Instead they live to a large extent in great organizations and a variety of voluntary associations. A congregation that roots in a residential neighborhood has a natural connection with only the home life of its members. And the downtown church is the religious association for its members with no natural community in which to root itself except the very vague loyalty to the city itself which its citizens may have. Thus the First Lutheran Church of Pittsburgh can say it represents Pittsburgh Lutheranism—but how strong or significant a tie is that in actual fact? The point is this: to reach people —Christian laymen or the unchurched—in their meaningful activities and associations, there must be other forms of church life beyond the congregations. Some of these new forms have emerged under the impetus of the lay renaissance.

This movement is by no means confined to Protestantism. For several decades Roman Catholicism has shown a renewed concern about an active role for laymen in the life of its church. That role is increasingly defined as relating the church (the spiritual order) to society (the temporal order) or the task of carrying Christian influences into the structures of modern society. The phrase "the lay apostolate" represents this idea, which has inspired a host of organizations, both in Europe and in America. These are known as "Catholic Action." One Catholic journalist describes the role of the Catholic laymen in America under the title of *The Emerging Layman*.[2]

Actually both Roman Catholic and Protestant laymen have been quite active in expressing their faith through most of the history of the United States. Especially within Protestantism lay movements have taken shape from time to time. An obvious example is that of the YMCA and the

[2] Donald J. Thorman, *The Emerging Layman* (Garden City, Doubleday, 1962). For a further description of lay movements among American Roman Catholics, see Leo R. Ward, *Catholic Life USA* (St. Louis, B. Herder, 1959).

YWCA. There have also been earlier forms of church organization similar to those which now express the lay renaissance. For example, Chautauquas and summer camps somewhat resemble the newer lay centers. But the lay renaissance carries a fresh and deeper meaning for the present age. Influenced by Europeans with their sense of crisis and penetrating theological insights, the lay renaissance seeks to show how Christians can be the church within the complexities of modern social struggles and within the crosscurrents of contemporary intellectual ferment. Of course, new forms can at best hope to be more relevant channels for the same precious story, the Gospel, and for the same unchanging power of God through his Holy Spirit. Ever-changing forms must emerge in each new day to carry the abiding resources of the Christian message into the hearts and lives of contemporary men.

A Variety of Experiments

In order to provide resources for the Christian's ministry in the world, and in order to represent the church at places where it is hardly to be found, a number of creative ventures have taken place in recent years. Some have been denominationally sponsored, but it is obvious that they serve their purpose according to their ability to serve all the laymen at a particular place and to represent the whole church (or at least Protestantism). In fact, the whole lay renaissance has helped to make it clear that the great Ecumenical Movement must find grass-roots expression in interdenominational co-operation, including an enlarged role for local councils and the National Council of Churches, as well as the World Council of Churches.

Many of these ventures can be called parachurches. A parachurch is a representation of the church which takes shape in an unconventional, nongeographic situation. It may be a clergyman or groups of laymen. It may have worship services and Bible study, like a congregation, or it may not. If it takes shape where Christians are naturally present, it will likely take on some of the activities of a regular congregation. Many chaplaincies do this, for example, in the armed services, at university campuses, or at resort spots during the recreation season. A church college could be considered a parachurch. Some parachurches reach out more radically by gathering the Christians in a given factory or a particular slum area or among a minority or depressed group who are unchurched. The hope is that outsiders, those who would not venture into a church building, may be drawn into a Christian fellowship within their own familiar surroundings.

The house-churches formed by some congregations also serve this purpose. For example, a mission congregation in Chicago's changing "South Side" moved out of its storefront through its "Operation Apartment." This operation included "open houses" held in many apartment buildings by church members who invited their neighbors in for coffee and talk about the community and the church's role in it. A few mission congregations (for example, the Lutheran Church in Cape Coral, Florida) have planted themselves within a shopping area to show that the church wishes to serve at the heart of the community. The Sheffield Industrial Mission (described in Chapter IX) serves the same purpose in a more sustained way, and on a deeper level.

More offbeat is the ministry of John Gensel to the jazz people of Greenwich Village in New York City. He is a pastor of a Lutheran congregation who is assigned half-time to this extracongregational work. Wearing a clerical collar, he spends most nights visiting the jazz night clubs, drinking Cokes and mingling with the patrons, but especially talking to the musicians, listening to their problems, expressing his own genuine appreciation of their art form as an authentic expression of modern life. He has learned a great deal about these musicians and about the tensions and separations under which they live. Here is the church listening to people and identifying with a segment of contemporary society usually remote from church circles. Perhaps he can discover or help to create Christian jazzmen who will learn to minister to the jazz world.

Cells of Christians are taking shape within the associations and organizations of modern secular life. Composed of people who belong to the same work situation or face the same problems, such cells are a more hopeful resource for the layman's ministry than are the small groups that form within congregations. They can be more directly and specifically helpful. One can get greater support from the fellow Christians who know concretely what he faces. In such a group he can confront complex issues with greater understanding, receive realistic suggestions, perhaps move with others in solving certain problems or in changing a given situation.

Such cells can form and are forming within factories, offices, labor unions, university departments, and many other workplaces or professional groups. Or businessmen may gather once a week for breakfast, for prayer, and for discussion. A car pool is a likely group for forming a cell. Ralston Young, a porter at Grand Central Station in New York City, has even formed a prayer group in an unused railroad car. Some of the larger German Evangelical Academies have had eighty or ninety such cells (already mentioned in Chapter IX), composed of "alumni" or former participants, scattered through the cities of their territory. They use full-time staff members to cultivate these groups, feeling that these are the best part of the follow-up from the Academy conferences.

Another worth-while trend is the increase of Christian professional associations or guilds. These are often national organizations within a given occupation. They may be well organized with national conventions and local chapters, with their own literature and study programs. Some of them may even try to influence policy within their general professional organization in the direction of Christian purposes. In any case they are most effective when they seek to enhance the leadership and influence of Christians within the general professional association rather than to divert their members from such participation. There is a Faculty Christian Fellowship, an Episcopal Guild of Scholars, an Episcopal Actors' Guild, and a Lutheran Nurses Guild. In New York there is a St. George Association for civil-service workers. In Philadelphia Protestant policemen are organized into the Legion of Cornelius. There are others, though this type of grouping needs to be greatly increased among Protestants. Roman Catholics have made greater progress, having, for example, an association of Catholic Trade Unionists, a Catholic Actors Guild, a Catholic Court Attachés' Guild, a Catholic Newsmen's Guild, and a Guild of Catholic Doctors. By developing such groups, Christian laymen can take a significant step toward relating their faith to their daily work.

Lay Centers

However, it is the lay centers which are the focal points for the lay renaissance. These are conference and retreat centers with two purposes, paralleling the two thrusts of the movement itself, namely, (1) to train laymen for their ministry in the world and (2) to be the church's place of dialogue with a society that is both secular and complex. In North America there are perhaps two dozen Protestant lay centers. Among the best known are these: Parishfield (Brighton, Michigan), the Faith and Life Community (Austin, Texas), Packard Manse (Stoughton, Massachusetts),

Five Oaks (Paris, Ontario), Kirkridge (Bangor, Pennsylvania), Yokefellow House (Richmond, Indiana), Wainwright House (Rye, New York), Thompson House (Webster Groves, Missouri), and Pendle Hill (Wallingford, Pennsylvania).

We have already described some of the Dutch centers, Sigtuna in Sweden (see Chapter VIII), the Evangelical Academies in Germany, and something about the lay center in Ontario called Five Oaks (see Chapter IX). The centers in North Anerica are not so large nor so well established as those in Europe. Their financial support is often precarious and their staffs are small. Their mood is one of searching and experimentation, though several are about twenty years old. Yet their leaders sense that they are responding to God's call by answering a deep need and they are convinced that the Holy Spirit speaks with power through their witness. A booklet describing the European lay centers is entitled *Signs of Renewal;* the American centers are also signs of renewal, though on a more humble scale at present.

What is a lay center? It is a *Christian conference center* which seeks to *prepare laymen* for their *ministries* in the *world.* Each italicized word needs explanation.

It is *Christian,* rooting itself in the Christian faith and tradition and relating itself in a variety of specific ways to the life of the contemporary Christian Church, its denominations, and its organizations.

It is a *center,* a place with facilities for people to live and study together. Typically it is also a community of people, often several families, who live together in Christian fellowship and with some sharing of physical facilities. It has its own atmosphere in appearance, daily routine, and communal patterns. It provides leadership, often resident clergymen, for the conferences and groups of people that gather at that place.

Its work usually consists in large part of *conferences.* An-

nually its program schedule will include a number of two-
or three-day meetings for visitors with a common interest
—an announced theme, the same occupation, or a particular congregation. The activities of a given conference may
include a few speeches, serious Bible study, extended and
informal discussion, and participation in the resident community's life of worship, eating, fellowship, and household
chores. Retreats and more formal courses also have their
places in many lay centers.

Its work is primarily with *laymen* whose occupations are
not within the organized church but in "secular" society.
This does not exclude ordained ministers and other full-
time workers in church organizations, but the emphasis lies
upon the great bulk of Christians who are otherwise employed.

It seeks to *prepare* the layman for his Christian responsibilities. Such preparation is usually conceived in broad
terms. It includes study and training and spiritual renewal
and personal encounter. It intends to be existential, concrete, informal yet intense, experience-oriented, open and
permissive, rather than dogmatic, yet grappling with Christian truth. Without ignoring intellectual encounter, it endeavors to touch the whole of life by using group dynam-
ics, Christian fellowship, and the whole pattern of life
together to bring definite personal meaning to the total conference experience.

Many lay centers stress the renewal of the church and
seek to open participants to a fresh incursion of the Holy
Spirit. They would be "the breeding-places of a new type
of alerted and alert Christians," as Hendrik Kraemer has
described the Evangelical Academies.

The lay center is concerned primarily with the layman's
existence in the *world* rather than in the organized church
or in his interior life. This distinguishes the lay center from

many other retreat and lay training programs. Most frequently the lay center will set its themes and guide its discussion to start from a serious encounter with today's world, with the daily-life experience of participants, moving from the issues of a secular society to the central concerns of life under the Gospel. Thus occupational or issue-centered conferences are popular. These conferences will ask what Christian obedience means within a specific professional or technical situation, what a Christian is and does within the particular context which frames the daily existence of the participants.

A lay center seeks to train laymen for their *ministries* within the secular spheres of today's world. If the church carries Christ's ministry within the modern world, then laymen as integral parts of the People of God carry that ministry wherever they go. Their major ministry will lie beyond the structures of the organized church. The lay center helps laymen to be the church within the rest of society, the church dispersed into every area of human life. Believing that all facets of the organized church should work more pointedly toward this end, lay center leaders nonetheless bear this particular calling and task in our day, and *lay centers carry this distinctive function.*

A description of one center will illustrate. Parishfield is a study center of the Protestant Episcopal Church at Brighton, Michigan. Though it is nurtured within one denomination, its concerns and most of its conferences are interdenominational.

What was a pleasant farm twenty years ago is now the little Christian community of Parishfield. The buildings have been modernized and altered, but they remain clearly farm buildings. Two efficient dormitories could be chicken houses. The central barn is still a barn, yet also clearly a chapel with a cross upon its peak. Parishfield thus symbolizes its firm belief that worship and daily work must be closely joined.

Composed of three resident families and a score or more laymen or laywomen who join the community for a weekend or a month, Parishfield is dedicated to the training of laity for their vocation as Christians. Since 1949 its founders, Episcopal clergymen Francis Ayers and Gibson Winter (now at the University of Chicago), have experimented in finding ways of preparing devout laymen to witness to Christ amid the routine of their day-by-day lives.

Certain methods have shown themselves to be trustworthy. Worship is a central and intense experience in the community's life. As the members of the group gather about the altar, which stands in the middle of the modernistic chapel, they not only renew their awareness of the source of life but also come to realize something of the moment-by-moment purpose of living and toiling.

Bible study takes up most of the morning. Selected passages are first carefully studied by each individual and then thoughtfully discussed in small, earnest groups. Meaning and relevance are sought for daily work and decisions.

When Dick Leonard (see the opening paragraphs of this book) attended Parishfield several years ago, his fellow participants discussed with him—in the light of God's Word —his on-the-job problems as a Christian who repairs typewriters and business machines. He helped to thrash through the issues that confronted two of the girls in the group who are Protestant nurses and not always in agreement with the procedures of their superiors in a Roman Catholic hospital. There was much talk, for instance, of the tension between the need to obey authority in a large, tightly interrelated hospital and the need to obey one's own conscience.

Parishfield leaders, while loving and serving the church, at one time stated that "the superficiality of most of its fellowship is the greatest weakness of the church today." They emphasize the experience of living in a Christian community for the training of laymen. Parishfield illustrates this, creating an atmosphere of fellowship and trust that provides background for the frank and deep discussions.

The conference groups move together at work and at leisure, use first names only, and come to know each other well even in a brief period. Most of the cooking is done by the participants, as is all of the cleaning and KP work. Everyone spends at least an hour each morning working at other tasks necessary to maintaining the center's physical facilities. "Wholeness of Christian life" is given meaning in the Parishfield program.

There are no glittering statistical successes to report about this enterprise in Michigan. Yet it has had a quietly leavening influence in a number of directions. Beyond its conferences it has gone through several phases of specialized efforts. In one phase Parishfield leaders patiently gathered men and women of a particular occupation, drawn mostly from Detroit's industry, to spend a long weekend twice a year in study and discussion of the meaning of the Gospel for that occupation and for the situation in which these people work. Thus there have been groups of executives, supervisors, union officials, production workers, and office workers. This is a significant front-line activity for the modern Christian church in America.

Another facet of Parishfield's work has been prolonged discussion of a modern Christian style of life.[3] Most recently, deciding that modern life has become so privatized that people dangerously ignore their public responsibilities, Parishfield leaders are seeking to serve directly the public life of Detroit, especially its urban renewal proj-

[3] Francis O. Ayres has drawn upon this discussion and study in writing *The Ministry of the Laity* (Philadelphia, Westminster, 1962). The present writer is also indebted at many points to Parishfield.

ects and its work in the correction and prevention of crime. Part of the Parishfield staff now resides in that city. Thus this pioneering lay center continues to experiment and to challenge both church and society in modern America.

Most of the conference centers provide for some kind of follow-up with participants, a newsletter being a typical example. More important, some of the centers involve a minority of their participants in an ongoing disciplined fellowship.

The Yokefellows, for instance, are much more than a conference center. They are a goodly fellowship scattered throughout much of the United States. Under the inspiration of Elton Trueblood, well-known religious writer and professor at Earlham College, they have developed a common discipline—of time and talent and money and mind—that seeks to buttress the membership for the demands of daily Christian living. Each member wears as a lapel pin a small yoke to indicate that he is yoked to Christ in discipleship and mission. The pin also invites questions and an opportunity to bear witness.

Near Bangor, Pennsylvania, is the retreat and conference center called Kirkridge. On 350 acres in the Appalachians several buildings house some three dozen retreaters during each weekend throughout most of the year. Here at one time young mothers will retreat, at another time artists, at another seminarians, often simply those interested in a prayer week or a book study or church renewal. These are work retreats including manual labor, silence, worship, and discussion.

Begun in 1942 by an interdenominational group seeking to integrate Christian "social radicals" with "devotional radicals," Kirkridge is also a fellowship, headed by Yale Professor John Oliver Nelson and guided by a board of directors. With no formal membership and no lengthy resi-

dence at Kirkridge, this community includes more than
one hundred people who follow its "Discipline" or "Rule" and
report their progress from their scattered homes.

A recent form of the discipline of Kirkridge, now called
"The Style-Of-Life," reads like this:

1. *Prayer* At least a half hour daily in private devotion using
   the Kirkridge or other lectionary. Wherever possible this
   basic period should be early in the morning. It is supple-
   mented with family worship, devotional reading, grace at
   meals, and flash prayers for persons, causes, and praise.

2. *Identification* Specific sharing with persons suffering by prej-
   udice, pain, poverty, or unwisdom to bring unobtrusive compassion and strength for new life. Responsibility for others
   in personal habits. Practice of redemptive nonviolence.

3. *Study* Reading for intellectual growth and a sounder understanding of the faith that is within us the equivalent of at
   least a solid book monthly, to interpret past and present in
   Christian maturity.

4. *Stewardship* Drastic disciplining of time, energy and money
   so that ample and increasing margins may be available for
   deepest concerns.

5. *Church* Responsibility in the life and work of a local congregation and in the wider Christian fellowship.

6. *Nurture Group* Regular participation with a few others of
   similar purpose in study, prayer, sharing of problems and
   experience with this or other style-of-life.

7. *Retreat* Withdrawal at least annually with other Kirkridgers
   where possible, and monthly for two or more hours alone;
   to regain Christian perspective in silence and worship, and
   to review and renew priorities.

8. *Support of Kirkridge* In prayer, inviting, and annual financial contribution.

Are These Tomorrow's Patterns?

Are these lay training centers, together with the accompanying guilds, fellowships, and cells, a significant pattern for the future of the organized church? It is hard to predict. They have arisen spontaneously and haphazardly. No one has developed any master plan or over-all strategy. One would like to hail these directors of lay centers as the army engineers who move out under enemy fire before the infantry attack to repair the roads and throw up the bridges. And they are doing some of this. But it is not at all clear that the generals are going to mount the attack!

Even among those who have sensed that lay centers have a significant role to play in the church life of the coming decades, there are differences in judgment as to the specific place of these centers within the church's many organizations. Some people would hold that lay centers are mainly auxiliary to the congregations, a new way of improving the functioning of the present congregations by helping to inspire and train their leaders. Others find that the presence of lay centers poses more basic questions for the churches. These reflect two viewpoints, the first more radical in its questions than the second.

One group of critics of today's church takes a radical stance to ask this question: Do not these centers challenge the congregations and threaten to replace them as the way God will speak his Word to men in the latter part of the twentieth century? German sociologist Helmut Schelsky claims that truth can come to modern men only after lengthy inner, self-conscious reflection. This will mean, he believes, that real faith and firm decision will await prolonged discussion and dialogue between various ideas. Thus the indispensable modern institution is some organized opportunity for discussion, and all other social institutions will be subordinated to it. For churches this means that the discussion room (or the conference center) will replace the chapel at the heart of the church building and at the crucial points in church life.

Eberhard Mueller of the Bad Boll Academy has declared that alongside Word and Sacraments as pillars of the contemporary church must be placed Discussion. The idea is that God speaks to the "other-directed" modern man as that man talks back and forth (dialogues) with his fellow Christians. People with this viewpoint often declare the task of lay centers to be that of recovery of the Gospel itself. They understand lay centers to be the great new fact for the churches in this century and believe that the sorely needed renewal of the church can come only as all the traditional forms of congregational and denominational life are restructured in ways not yet discernible.

A second viewpoint is more tempered yet still seriously challenging. Its advocates are asking, Will not lay centers become a significant new structure within the churches, paralleling present congregations and providing needed services that local congregations cannot provide? Whereas parishes or congregations have largely served laymen in two facets of their lives, religion and the family, lay centers will serve laymen in the world, i.e., in the common or public life, in all of life beyond the other two areas.

True, lay centers will likely serve as the real spiritual home (the congregation) for some of the most mobile or transient of modern men, providing perhaps a week of retreat each year at a familiar place and with a familiar resident community. For many other people the centers will provide resources that will make them better members of their own congregations. But the main purpose of the center is to serve as the church's arm extended toward the world in which laymen live and work daily. Men think and act in groups in our day; better than congregations, centers can address such groups, gather them for encounter with Christian truth, and train the Christian toward living a Christian style of life within his own particular groups.

This second viewpoint commends itself, at least as a hope for the coming decades. The fulfillment of that hope will require the multiplication of lay training centers. Some of these centers should seek to involve the most influential people in American public life. Many more of them would be regional in their influence. Some centers would develop a broad program for many different groups of people. Others would specialize in conferences for a particular occupation or a particular sphere of culture.

Church colleges could become bases for the development of regional lay training centers. In these colleges many of the departments already have valuable, continuing contacts with alumni in various occupations (for example, teaching, nursing, music, medicine, industrial research, law, business, government). Such contacts could be developed into occupational conferences for the training of Christian laymen. Universities, of course, represent greater centers of influence. Franklin Littell in *The German Phoenix* (Garden City, Doubleday, 1960) suggests that American Christians should carry the lay renaissance idea into the adult-education or extension programs of the great universities. This would be a much more difficult undertaking.

If lay centers are to increase, it will require that God raise up imaginative and discerning leaders for such centers. It will take some over-all, interdenominational co-ordination. It will take much vision on the part of ecclesiastical leaders and much patient co-operation on the part of pastors of congregations.

Above all, if lay centers are to assume such a prophetic role within American Christianity, they will have to call forth and help to create a new brand of laymen who will be ready to be trained, who will with vision and dedication move into their daily tasks as a ministry in Christ's name.

Epilogue

AGENTS OF RECONCILIATION

The layman who has read the foregoing pages may readily come to the end with a feeling of discouragement or dismay. Servants serve, light reveals, salt redeems, soldiers resist evil, and militant churchmen restructure their organization. Can the ordinary man's ministry encompass all this?

Without doubt the layman's ministry in the world is difficult. The roles of servant and soldier are exacting and costly. The gifts of light and salt make burdensome demands upon their bearers. Nor will a reorientation of the institutional church be accomplished without friction and loss.

Then let it be quickly underscored: *We are not called upon to succeed.* No victory has been promised to us. We are simply expected to be faithful with our God-given gifts and tasks. Nor are we God's only agents. He works through all of history in mysterious ways. We do not even understand much that he does. We have been given a ministry in Christ's name and we trust that God will use us as he sees fit.

Only Christ can bring the victory. His coming in power will be that victory, and our waiting and trying will be caught up in a vastly greater triumph. There is not even any assurance that our small gains will have an organic connection with the final breaking in of the Kingdom. They are, nonetheless, signs of what God is bringing to pass in his own time and way.

And they are our responses to his grace. Let it also be quickly underlined: *We do not minister in our own power.* Faced with such responsibilities, anyone might wonder why such a mantle has fallen on him. What right has a tradesman, housewife, salesman, teacher,

farmer, student, or lawyer to presume to act for God? The same right
accorded the Prodigal Son when he was received home by the waiting
father. The father quickly restored to him the high privileges of an
heir. "Put the best robe upon his shoulders": let him wear my colors
with pride. "Put the ring upon his hand": let him act for me, and I
will stand behind his actions with my resources and the majestic
power of my name.[1]

However, when one asks what God may actually be doing with and
through our ministry for this world which he loves, there are only
hints of an answer. It has already been suggested that we bear light
and salt which can reveal God and redeem the world. But God's
central purpose is to *reconcile*, to bring men and the world back into
right relationship to him. We are agents of reconciliation.[2] We carry
the message of the King's pardon and renewed favor to those who
have been banished from him. "God was in Christ reconciling the
world to himself . . . and entrusting to us the message of reconciliation" (II Cor. 5:19).

What God does through us is not so much to transfigure or to
transform but to *confront* men. We are the agents of God bringing men
to the point of decision. God does the confronting; they do the deciding for or against him. *We provoke the crisis*, in keeping with the
promise made to Abraham that through his posterity decision would
be forced upon "all the families of the earth" (Gen. 12:3).

Both the role of suffering servant and that of soldier provoke crisis
in those served or opposed. The gifts we bear have the same quality.
Light arouses conflict with darkness, as John's Gospel makes clear.
Salt irritates the cut and hastens the issue.

Salt also makes men thirsty and aware of their need to drink. The
intense mutual concern within our Christian fellowship and the expendable love which we pour out upon other men so amaze and
irritate them as to evoke their questions concerning the hope that
is in us and to arouse their thirst for the good news that intoxicates
us.

Thus we raise up signs and are ourselves signs that crisis is upon
men today. We bring to the world discernment, the ability to dis-

[1] This idea is expressed by J. Bruce Weaver in *The Lutheran*, January 24,
1962, p. 15.
[2] This is the theme worked out in Arnold B. Come, *Agents of Reconciliation* (Philadelphia, Westminster, 1960).

tinguish good and evil, forcing decision. What was dull gray is now
sharply etched in black and white. What was bland has become
biting. Antichrist and Christ stand forth locked in battle. These are
troubled times, heavy with threats. For us they are also "the birth-
pangs of the new age" (Matt. 24:8, New English translation), so that
in the midst of pain we look forward with a steady hope. Today
those fateful words "Choose you this day" come with greater urgency
for more people over wider portions of the globe than ever before.

Many revolutions are let loose in our time. The first Christians were
themselves thought of as ones to overturn the world (Acts 17:6).
Actually the Gospel has had a hand in creating the ferment that has
produced this revolutionary age. The real spirit of revolution, as
Jacques Ellul points out, affirms a spiritual truth in the face of the
"facts" and the hard ideology of the moment.[3]

Here is our call, as twentieth-century Christians, to be the *true*
revolutionaries. Not card carrying but *torchbearing*, the ones who appear at a turning point in history and force the issue—firebrands, if
you please. Not troublemakers bent on tearing things up. Not with
blasts of judgment upon others; we, too, are in the crisis, for the
torches light up the grotesque features of our own faces and we may
be burned by them (I Cor. 3:13). Not hoping to rise to the top of
the heap with new power through violence. We are only agents; we
help the rightful King confront his subjects face to face asking for a
clear decision.

This story by Paul C. Empie, executive director of the National
Lutheran Council and administrator of overseas relief, sums it up well.
This *is* God's world and He *is* sovereign, Dr. Empie reminds us. "God's
will is going to be done, through us, if we are usable, through others
if we are not. A few years ago I visited in Spain a small Protestant
hostel for boys in the mountains north of Madrid. The main building
had been a monastery; behind it was a courtyard in the middle of
which was an old millstone. Years ago someone had planted a tree
in the hole in the center of the millstone, and it had grown until it
had filled the hole. Little by little the stone began to squeeze into the
bark and people expected this lovely shade tree to be choked to death.
One morning the pastor walked by and noted that the tree had split
the stone! God is like that. Quietly, His Spirit and His will penetrate

[3] Jacques Ellul, *The Presence of the Kingdom* (Philadelphia, Westminster,
1951), Olive Wyon, trans., p. 40.

the crevices and the cracks of society and the revolutionary explosion is accompanied both by judgment and redemption."[4]

[4] From a speech by Paul C. Empie at Minneapolis, June 14, 1962, printed as "Christian World Mission in World Revolution" by Lutheran World Action (New York, National Lutheran Council), p. 20.

SUGGESTIONS FOR FURTHER READING

SECTION ONE

Brown, Robert McAfee, *The Significance of the Church* (Philadelphia, The Westminster Press, 1956).

de Dietrich, Suzanne, *The Witnessing Community* (Philadelphia, The Westminster Press, 1958).

Heiges, Donald R., *The Christian's Calling* (Philadelphia, Muhlenberg Press, 1958).

Herberg, Will, *Protestant-Catholic-Jew* (Garden City, Doubleday & Co., 1956).

Kraemer, Hendrik, *A Theology of the Laity* (Philadelphia, The Westminster Press, 1958).

Laity, Bulletin of the Departments on the Laity and on the Co-operation of Men and Women (Geneva, World Council of Churches), issued semiannually.

Marty, Martin, *The New Shape of American Religion* (New York, Harper & Bros., 1959).

Miller, Donald G., *The Nature and Mission of the Church* (Richmond, Va., John Knox Press, 1957).

Spike, Robert W., *In But Not Of The World* (New York, Association Press, 1957).

Trueblood, Elton, *Your Other Vocation* (New York, Harper & Bros., 1952).

SECTION TWO

Ayres, Francis O., *The Ministry of the Laity* (Philadelphia, The Westminster Press, 1962).

Bonhoeffer, Dietrich, *Prisoner for God* (New York, The Macmillan Co., 1958).

Forell, George W., *Ethics of Decision* (Philadelphia, Muhlenberg Press, 1955).

Kee, Howard Clark, *Making Ethical Decisions* (Philadelphia, The Westminster Press, 1957).

Lewis, C. S., *Christian Behaviour* (New York, The Macmillan Co., 1945).

Pike, James A., *Doing the Truth* (Garden City, Doubleday & Co., 1956).

SECTION THREE

Dexter, Harriet Harmon, *What's Right with Race Relations* (New York, Harper & Bros., 1958).

Klausler, Alfred P., *Christ and Your Job* (St. Louis, Concordia Publishing House, 1956).

Living My Religion on My Job, study book published by the Laymen's Movement for a Christian World, Rye, N.Y., 1962.

Miller, Alexander, *Christian Faith and My Job* (New York, Association Press, 1946).

Miller, William Lee, *The Protestant and Politics* (Philadelphia, The Westminster Press, 1958).

Muehl, William, *Mixing Religion and Politics* (New York, Association Press, 1958).

Spike, Robert W., *To Be a Man* (New York, Association Press, 1961).

Spurrier, William A., *Ethics and Business* (New York, Charles Scribner's Sons, 1962).

Taylor, Richard, *Christians in an Industrial Society* (London, SCM Press, 1961).

SECTION FOUR

Bonhoeffer, Dietrich, *The Cost of Discipleship* (New York, The Macmillan Co., 1957).

Casteel, John L., ed., *Spiritual Renewal Through Personal Groups* (New York, Association Press, 1957).

Frakes, Margaret, *Bridges to Understanding* (Philadelphia, Muhlenberg Press, 1960).

Grimes, Howard, *The Rebirth of the Laity* (New York, Abingdon Press, 1962).

Littell, Franklin H., *The German Phoenix* (Garden City, Doubleday & Co., 1960).

Morton, T. Ralph, *Community of Faith* (New York, Association Press, 1954).

Raines, Robert A., *New Life in the Church* (New York, Harper & Bros., 1961).

Religion in Life (Nashville, Abingdon Press), Winter, 1961–62, (symposium on the lay renaissance).

Shands, Alfred R., *The Liturgical Movement and the Local Church* (London, SCM Press, 1959).

Signs of Renewal (Geneva, World Council of Churches, 1957), Hans-Ruedi Weber, ed.

Southcott, Ernest W., *The Parish Comes Alive* (New York, Morehouse-Gorham Co., 1957).

Trueblood, Elton, *The Company of the Committed* (New York, Harper, & Bros., 1961).

Union Seminary Quarterly Review (New York, Union Theological Seminary, 3041 Broadway, New York 27, N.Y.), March 1961 (six congregations report on renewal).

Webber, George W., *God's Colony in Man's World* (New York, Abingdon Press, 1960).